# THE DEVELOPMENT
# OF CHRISTIANITY
# IN THE LATIN
# CARIBBEAN

# THE DEVELOPMENT OF CHRISTIANITY IN THE LATIN CARIBBEAN

*by*

JUSTO L. GONZÁLEZ

WILLIAM B. EERDMANS PUBLISHING COMPANY
GRAND RAPIDS, MICHIGAN

# EDITORIAL FOREWORD

*Christian World Mission Books* treat every aspect of the world mission of the Church of Christ — history, theory, methods, functional approaches, regional studies, biography, and collections of source material. One purpose is to make available knowledge about the mission to the growing number of readers who are discovering the importance of the mission in cultural interchange and international relations. Another purpose is to provide students and churchmen with the literature needed for their studies of the mission. The authors are recruited from many nations and churches. They include ecumenical and evangelical Protestants, Roman Catholics, and eventually, it is hoped, Orthodox. The books may contribute to unity for mission and to the dialogue on what mission is in the new era just opening.

The first two series are devoted to history. This is because one historical era has just ended and another is beginning, making urgent a review of the first. The old era of missions, both in Roman Catholic and Protestant Churches, was a unilateral *sending* operation out of Western Christendom into the rest of the world. Now a new era of "world mission" begins. The first series of *Christian World Mission Books* is "The Churches in Mission," and treats the development of the sending mission out of each of the Western nations or regions. The second series is "Discipling the Nations," and deals with the history of the missions and the resulting churches in the various fields. The present volume by Dr. Justo L. González, professor in the union Evangelical Seminary of Puerto Rico and an eminent historian, brings the Roman Catholic and Protestant aspects of mission history in the Latin Caribbean together into a single introductory volume. This is the first book in the series.

R. PIERCE BEAVER
*Editor*

# TABLE OF CONTENTS

CONTENTS

# PART ONE

# CHRISTIANITY UNDER
# THE COLONIAL REGIME

# I

# A NEW WORLD FOR A NEW SPAIN

¡Tierra! Land ho! cried an excited voice aboard Their Catholic Majesties' ship *La Pinta*. For that man, as well as for his other companions aboard the three Spanish caravels, that cry was the end of five weeks of ever increasing anxiety. For their admiral it was the culmination of years of planning, scheming, and begging in European courts. But for Spain it was to become the threshold of its path to historical greatness.

Just a few years earlier Spain was a handful of kingdoms and counties in which Christian and Muslim almost constantly fought each other, with brief respites during which they fought among themselves. That very year of 1492, a few months before the New World was discovered, the united kingdoms of Castille and Aragón had managed to conquer Granada, thereby destroying the last bulwark of Moorish power on the Peninsula.

Even then Spain was far from being united under the Christian faith. On the contrary there still remained strong Muslim and Jewish minorities. In 1492 Their Catholic Majesties ordered that every Jew who refused to be baptized must leave Spain. Although many Jews were baptized, the question immediately arose of the sincerity of their conversion. This in turn required the offices of the Inquisition, one of whose functions was to uncover those among the "new Christians" who in truth were still Jews. The people's hatred for the *marranos* — "pigs," as they called the converted Jews — was ever greater, and many of them fled to other parts of Europe and northern Africa.

The Muslim population was concentrated in the South. According to the terms of Granada's surrender, their religion would be tolerated. And for a few years it was so, until the zealous reformer Cardinal Ximenes de Cisneros, taking this to be a sign of weakness, tried to force the conversion of all Muslims. The several rebellions that ensued were violently crushed. In 1524 Charles V ordered that every Muslim who refused to be baptized should be expelled from Spain. With these measures the number of *moriscos* — converted Moors — began to increase, and the Inquisition began to seek out the false Christians among them. Finally, in 1567, Philip II ordered that the *moriscos* must abandon their peculiar customs and language, and become totally assimilated into the mainstream of Spanish culture.

The surprising fact about all this is that even before achieving the total assimilation of the Muslim and Jewish elements within her population, Spain plunged into the venture of taking her power, faith, and culture to a land many times larger than herself. The first half of the sixteenth century witnessed an unprecedented outpouring in which Spain flooded the New World. The reasons for this are subject to conjecture and speculation, but we can at least say that Spain came to the New World with three motivations that were able to unite the most dissimilar spirits in a common adventure: glory, gold, and religion. Those whose ambition was for glory and renown saw in the New World the occasion to explore and conquer lands even then unknown to them. Those who merely wished to get rich were attracted by the legends of the great treasures to be had in the "Indies." Finally, the existence of vast territories not yet evangelized attracted those for whom religion was the central motivation in their lives, especially the members of the regular orders.

The expansion of Spain in the New World during the sixteenth century is surprising. In 1492 Columbus set foot for the first time in these lands. In 1496 he founded the city of Santo Domingo de Guzmán on the island that he called Hispaniola. Only four years later Juan de la Cosa published the first map of the new lands. At that same time the northern coast of South America and a great section of North America were being explored. In 1508 Sebastián de Ocampo circumnavigated the island of Cuba, and thereby proved that it was not part of the mainland. The expedition of Vasco Núñez de Balboa, from 1509 to 1515, discovered the Pacific Ocean. In 1513 don Juan Ponce de León landed in Florida, and two years later at the other extreme of the hemisphere Juan Díaz de Solís reached the Río de la Plata. The expeditions to the coast of North America and throughout the continent were many, but among them the most remarkable is that of Alvaro Núñez Cabeza de Vaca, who in the years 1528 to 1536 traversed the continent from Texas to the Pacific Ocean. A few years later Fernando de Soto reached the Mississippi from Florida. At the same time, in the southern part of the New World, Francisco de Orellana was exploring the basin of the Amazon. The main purpose of these explorations was to find a route to the Orient and to discover the rich treasures that the Indians were supposed to have. But a great deal must be credited to the spirit of adventure that took possession of the Spansh soul during the sixteenth century.

The explorers were followed by the *conquistadores*. The greater Antilles did not offer serious resistance to the Spanish thrust, and soon all their original inhabitants were under new masters. To serve as centers of operations for further explorations and conquest, the Spaniards founded cities in the Caribbean that still exist today. Besides Santo Domingo, to which reference has already been made, they founded the

city of Puerto Rico — today called San Juan — in 1508, Santiago de Cuba in 1514, and Havana in 1515. In 1519 Hernán
Cortés landed in Mexico, and two years later he had fully
subdued the Aztec Empire. After some failures the final
conquest of Peru was undertaken by Francisco Pizarro and
Diego Almagro. In two years they were masters of Cuzco.
From then on all the principal centers of precolombian
culture and civilization, with the exception of Yucatán, were
in Spanish hands. The conquest of Central America and
Yucatán began in 1523 and took less than twenty years. With
this, and with some minor expeditions in the Río de la
Plata, Paraguay, and North America, the Spaniards reached
the apex of their expansion in the New World. This had
been achieved in less than half a century.

As was to be expected, the discoverers and conquerors were
followed by the settlers. Their main purpose was not to
discover new lands, but to remain in a fixed place where they
could devote themselves to commerce, agriculture, and above
all, mining rich ores. It was this wave of Spanish settlers that
gave stability and permanence to the great conquests of the
sixteenth century. If Hernán Cortés or Francisco Pizarro
had not been followed by thousands of men — and, later,
women — who were willing to settle permanently in the conquered lands, one could well suppose that very soon the
original inhabitants, and especially those of very high civili-
zations, such as the Aztecs, the Mayas, and the Incas, would
have been able to rid themselves of the Spanish yoke.

In all phases of the Spanish occupation of the New World
the Church played a major role. It had been represented in
every major expedition since Columbus' second voyage.[1]

---

[1] Some have claimed that the priest Pedro de Arenas accompanied Columbus in his first voyage. This is doubtful. In his second voyage Columbus took with him several Franciscans and a Hieronymite. In 1516, it
was made mandatory for every ship leaving for the Indies to take at least
one missionary. The list of those who came to the New World is almost
endless. Cf. F. de Lejarza, "Contenido misional del Catálogo de Pasajeros
a Indias," *Missionalia Hispanica*, I (1944), 571-582, as well as the "Aviv-

Some of these priests — especially the seculars — believed that their mission was limited to ministering to the spiritual needs of Spaniards.[2] Some Spaniards even doubted the possibility of converting the Indians.[3] But from the very beginning there were others who answered this question by saying that it was not only possible, but that both the Church and the Spanish crown were charged with the responsibility of achieving such a conversion, and that precisely this was the main purpose of the conquest and colonization of the New World.[4]

In order to fulfill the vast missionary task that was set before her in the New World, Spain had as her main asset a profound religious spirit that had been developed through years of bitter struggle against the Muslim invaders. The most remarkable sign of this spirit, as well as the most useful tool that Spain had in attempting to fulfill her newly acquired missionary obligation, were the then flourishing orders of Franciscans[5] and Dominicans.[6] Besides, Spain was the birthplace of Ignacio de Loyola, and for that reason as well as others the Society of Jesus had developed deep roots and wide outreach in that country.[7] These orders — as well as

---

amiento y catálogo de misiones y misioneros que en el siglo XVI pasaron de España a Indias y Filipinas según los libros de la Contratación," which has been published in *Missionalia Hispanica.*

[2] Cf. C. Bayle, *El clero secular y la evangelización de América.*

[3] This subject will be discussed further on.

[4] King Ferdinand agreed with this when he wrote: "According to the obligation and charge which has made us Lord of the Indies and the states in the ocean, nothing do we wish more than the publication and expansion of the Gospel Law and the conversion of the Indians to our Holy Catholic Faith." Quoted in C. Bayle, "El campo propio del sacerdote secular en la evangelización americana," *Missionalia Hispanica,* III (1946), 469-470. See also C. Bayle, "Ideales misioneros de los Reyes Católicos," *Missionalia Hispanica,* IX (1952), 209-231.

[5] The bibliography regarding the Franciscans in Spanish America is enormous. There are many useful bibliographical notes in P. Borges, *Métodos misionales en la cristianización de América, siglo XVI,* pp. 13-23.

[6] See A. Figueres, "Principios de la expansión dominicana en Indias," *Missionalia Hispanica,* I (1944), 303-340.

[7] See F. Mateos, "Antecedentes de la entrada de los Jesuítas españoles

the Mercedarians[8] — were the main sources of manpower for missionary work by the Catholic Church in the new Spanish possessions.

On the other hand, the Spanish crown made extensive use of the powers given it by what is known as the *Patronato Real*. In a series of five bulls, all dated in 1493,[9] Alexander VI gave the kings of Spain political and religious authority over all lands discovered or to be discovered beyond a line of demarcation a hundred leagues west of the Azores, and as long as all sailing to them proceeded westward, and the territories themselves were not previously in the hands of some other Christian prince. This was not only a privilege granted Their Catholic Majesties — and naturally, the king of Portugal — but it was also a missionary charge laid upon them. In truth this was the way in which the popes of the Renaissance, more interested in the arts and humanities than in religion, laid upon the kings of Spain and Portugal what ought to have been their own missionary responsibility.[10]

---

en las misiones de América: 1538-1565," *Missionalia Hispanica,* I (1944), 109-166; F. Mateos, "Primera expedición de misioneros jesuítas al Perú," *Missionalia Hispanica,* II (1945), 41-108.

8 J. Castro Seoane, "La expansión de la Merced en la América colonial," *Missionalia Hispanica,* I (1944), 73-108; II (1945), 231-290; by the same author, "La Merced en el Perú," *Missionalia Hispanica,* III (1946), 243-320; IV (1947), 137-169 and 383-401; VII (1950), 55-80. Also H. Sancho de Sopranis, "Irradiación misionera del Convento de la Merced de Jerez," *Missionalia Hispanica,* XI (1954), 5-54.

9 F. Mateos, "Bulas portuguesas y españolas sobre descubrimientos geográficos," *Missionalia Hispanica,* XIX (1962), 5-34, 129-168. The bulls are entitled *Inter caetera, Eximiae devotionis,* second *Inter caetera, Piis fidelium,* and *Duum siquidem,* and their text can be found in F. J. Hernáez, *Colección de Bulas, Breves y otros documentos relativos a la Iglesia de América y Filipinas,* 2 vols. Naturally, as the Portuguese began travels of exploration before the Spaniards, the background of the Spanish *Patronato* is to be found in bulls related to Portugal. Later the wider concessions made by Rome to the Spanish crown led it to give to Portugal similar rights, known as the *Padroado.*

10 There are different interpretations of the relationship between King Ferdinand and Pope Alexander VI, and there are also therefore different understandings of the background and reasons for the various bulls of

Beginning in 1501, the Spanish treasury received the tithes of the new churches,[11] but it was also responsible for all the expenses of the missionary enterprise. Normally, the royal treasury devoted two-thirds of the tithes to help the parishes and dioceses in the New World, and the rest to works of charity. When the first episcopal sees were established, Pope Julius II granted to the kings of Spain the right to propose the names of those who they thought should occupy these and other ecclesiastical charges — what is usually called the right of presentation.[12]

Although the pontifical bulls referred to the function of the Spanish crown in the New World as a patronage, the rights granted thereby were so extensive that soon various Spanish theologians, in the New World as well as in the old country, developed the theory of the *Vicariato Regio,* which claimed that the king was the vicar of the Pope in the New World.[13]

This conjunction of the interests of the State with those of the expansion of Christianity could have been tragic, and it obviously was in certain cases. Missions were often used as a means to extend Spanish culture and power.[14] But on the

---

1493. On the one hand, see M. Giménez Fernández, "Nuevas considera-ciones sobre la historia y sentido de las letras alejandrinas de 1493 referentes a las Indias," *Anuario de Estudios Americanos,* I (Sevilla, 1944); and by the same author, "Todavía más sobre las letras alejandrinas de 1493 referentes a las Indias," *Anales de la Universidad Hispalense,* XIV (1953), 241-301. On the other hand, see V. D. Sierra, "En torno a las bulas alejandrinas de 1493," *Missionalia Hispanica,* X (1953), 73-122; and, by the same author, "Y nada más sobre las bulas alejandrinas de 1493," *Missionalia Hispanica,* XII (1955), 403-428.

11 Bull *Eximiae devotionis,* of Alexander VI. Text in Hernáez, *op. cit.,* I, 20-21.

12 *Universalis Ecclesiae,* 1508 (Hernáez, *op. cit.,* pp. 24-25).

13 The most exhaustive study of this theory is to be found in A. de Egaña, *La teoría del Regio Vicariato español en Indias.*

14 Legally, the opposite was true. According to the law, the Spaniards were to "request" the Indians to submit peacefully to missionary work — which in any case was also of a political nature — and there was to be no recourse to arms unless they refused to abide by such request. In practice

other hand, one should remember that the spirit of the times was such, and this union of Church and State was taken to be so natural, that one did not usually think, as the modern mentality often tends to interpret the situation, in terms of the State making use of the Church, or vice versa. For Their Catholic Majesties and their subjects, European culture — and especially Spanish culture — was synonymous with the Christian faith. Therefore the Hispanization and the Christianization of the American Indians were for them one and the same thing. Nor must we forget that the crown always tried to protect the Indians from every attempt to exploit or enslave them.[15] If such attempts did not, however, succeed, and if there were mass killings that remained unpunished, this was not due to the will of the kings, but to the enormous distance that made it difficult for them to have that will fully obeyed. When one studies the history of the Spanish colonization in the New World, one finds that in general the crown and the regular clergy stood side by side against the abuses of other Spaniards against the Indians, although sometimes the secular clergy did support some of the inhuman practices of the *conquistadores*.

Thus, in conquering the New World Spain took upon herself the charge to see that its inhabitants were duly Christianized, and her own Church and faith strongly implanted in her new possessions. How she attempted to do so, and in what measure she succeeded, will be seen in the next chapters.

the *Requerimiento* was often used as an excuse for armed conquest. See B. Biermann, "Das Requerimiento in der spanischen Conquista," *Neue Zeitschrift für Missionswissenschaft,* VI (1950), 94-114.

[15] L. Hanke, *The Spanish Struggle for Justice in the Conquest of America.* The text of some of the documents that prove this assertion can be seen in Hernáez, *op. cit.,* pp. 28-49.

# II

# THE METHODS

IN THE SPANISH EVANGELIZATION OF THE CARIBBEAN, IT WAS not the theory of mission that determined the methods, but vice versa. The inhabitants were so few (probably not more than 250,000), the conquest so rapid and overwhelming, and the vested interests so many and great that there was hardly any time or occasion to think calmly about the methods to be followed in the attempt to Christianize the Indians. In fact, whereas in Spain the missionary aspect of the colonial enterprise was always a determining factor in the minds of Ferdinand and Isabella, in the New World most of the Spaniards were primarily interested in quenching their thirst for conquest, gold, and glory. Given the enormous distance and the tardiness of communications between these two poles of Spanish interest, it was to be expected that the net result would be that the Spaniards in the New World would have their way, and that the crown would only be able to mitigate in a small measure the evils thus brought upon the Indian population.

This situation was evident from the very beginning of Columbus' occupation of Hispaniola. His methods of subduing the Indians were ruthless, and those who would not obey him were punished brutally. Many he sent as slaves to Spain. He claimed that his reason for this was to have them come in contact with Christian culture and thereby accept the faith. In truth he was simply using them as payment for the merchandise he received from the Peninsula.[1] Although this supposed missionary method was condemned partially by Queen Isabella, and was actually one of the reasons why Columbus and his brothers were deposed and taken back to Spain in chains, the evil had already been done. The Indians' mistrust toward the Spanish that had been fostered by Columbus' hard measures would remain for years one of the greatest obstacles in the missionary enterprise.

But Columbus also established another so-called missionary method which was to be approved by the Spanish crown, and which would remain in effect long after his dismissal and death: the *encomiendas.* According to this system a group of Indians was given in trust to a Spaniard, who was to teach them the Christian faith. In return for that service the Indians were to work for their *encomenderos.* Naturally, this was only a veiled form of slavery, for the Spaniards to whom the Indians had been entrusted were much more interested in obtaining the results of their work than in teaching them the fundamentals of Christianity. Also, as the Indians were not strictly their property, they were often treated worse than slaves, for their master had no great interest in keeping alive this commodity that could be replaced quite readily. Surprisingly enough, however, Queen Isabella was impressed by the evangelistic excuses for the *encomiendas,* and in 1503 gave them her legal sanction. Six years later King Ferdinand made the situation even more abusive by authorizing the Spanish settlers in Hispaniola to bring in Indians from other islands

---

[1] F. Zubillaga, in *Historia de la Iglesia en la América Española: desde el descubrimiento hasta comienzos del siglo XIX,* pp. 216-217.

in order to serve them and to be Christianized. This decree opened the way for what was in fact an active slave trade.[2]

As far as we know, the *encomiendas* received no active opposition during the first years of their existence. However, in 1511 Fray Antonio Montesinos, of the Dominican order, began a vigorous campaign against them. This was promptly taken up by the rest of the order, whose members refused to give absolution to those who had Indians entrusted to them and would not let them go. The debate was carried on to Spain, and the final result was the new legislation known as the *Ley de Burgos,* in 1512.[3] According to this law the Indians were not to be treated as slaves, and those entrusted to a settler could neither be sold nor transferred to another. Besides, their work was to receive its just wages.[4] As was to be expected, the *Ley de Burgos* was never faithfully applied in America, but it witnesses to the positive attitude of the crown toward the efforts of the Dominican friars to make the colonial regime more humane.

Another advocate of the Indians, much better known than Father Montesinos, was Bartolomé de Las Casas, who also joined the Dominican order. He himself had held *encomiendas* in Hispaniola and Cuba. But he gave them up, sold his property in the New World, and returned to Spain in order to seek laws that would guarantee more justice for the Indians. There he received the title of "General Protector of the Indians," and with it he returned to the Caribbean. However, the Spanish settlers, and even a large sector of the clergy, took him to be a dreamer who thought that the Indians were people like the rest, and that they could be pacified with mere love. Faced by the impossibility of having the new laws obeyed, Las Casas returned to Spain, and thereby began a life of constant travel across the Atlantic, taking upon himself the task of securing better laws from the authorities in Spain, and

---

[2] *Ibid.,* p. 255.

[3] *Ibid.,* pp. 256-257.

[4] R. Altamira, "El texto de las Leyes de Burgos de 1512," *Revista de Historia de América,* I (1938), 5-77.

of seeing that they were obeyed in the colonies. In America he traveled from Mexico to Peru, always with the same purpose in mind. His greatest triumph was the promulgation of the "New Laws" of 1542, which guaranteed certain rights and protection to the Indians. After being consecrated bishop of Chiapas, where his ministry was exemplary, Las Casas returned to Spain, where he died in 1566.[5]

Another missionary method that was employed first in the Caribbean, and later and with much greater success in Paraguay, was the establishment of *reducciones*. Apart from those of the higher civilization, most American Indians — and, certainly, all those of the Caribbean — lived scattered in the jungles, in small communities that seldom were more than a large family. This hindered their "Christianization," and made practically impossible the task of regulating and supervising their customs. For these reasons,[6] and with the support of the crown,[7] the friars often brought these groups together into a larger community, which they called *reducción* or

---

[5] The case of Las Casas is not unique in the history of Spanish America. On the contrary there were many missionaries who followed the same course of action. If we do not discuss their lives and work, it is because that would take us far beyond the scope of the Latin Caribbean. However, some of them must at least be mentioned in order to give the reader a clear idea of the scope of their action. In Mexico Bishop Zumárraga, a man of vast humanistic culture, distinguished himself for his work toward the general education and religious instruction of the Indians. It was he who established the first printing press in the New World. Bartolomé de Olmedo, Eusebio Kino, Luis Cancer, Luis Beltrán, and Francisco Solano are just a few among the many who devoted their whole lives to better the lot of the Indians. One must also point out that some of the civil authorities in the New World were very much concerned for the well-being of its original inhabitants — among them, the famous Cabeza de Vaca.

[6] See M. Merino, "La reducción de los indios a pueblos: Medio de Evangelización," *Missionalia Hispanica,* III (1946), 184. Borges, *Métodos misionales en la cristianización de América, siglo XVI,* pp. 216-219, gives ample proof of the evangelizing motivation in the establishment of the *reducciones.*

[7] The first laws in favor of the *reducciones* were enacted in 1503 (Borges, *op. cit.,* p. 219).

*misión.* The *reducción* was a small village built around the
church and the square next to it. Work in it was supervised
by the friars, who taught its inhabitants new methods of agriculture and handicrafts. At the same time they were in-
structed in the Christian faith and their customs were supervised in order to bring them more in line with what the
friars believed to be Christian. There is no doubt that these
*misiones* were a great deal better than the *encomiendas,* whose
only real result was the exploitation of the Indians. But the
*reducciones* also had their weak points, especially their excessive paternalism, which, after uprooting the Indians from
their old system of life, did not really prepare them to take
care of themselves within the new civilization and customs
that they had adopted. For these reasons many *misiones* disappeared as soon as, for one reason or another, the friars had
to abandon them.[8] In theory, as soon as the *reducciones* were
properly established, the friars would turn them over to the
secular clergy, and would then go on to the establishment of
new communities. In practice this seldom took place, for the
friars did not wish to leave their *reducciones,* and the secular
priests were not too interested in occupying parishes that
produced such small revenues.

The other method some friars followed in their missionary
task was to take in with them the children of some of the
chieftains in order to give them some of the intellectual tools
of European culture, as well as a basic knowledge of the
Christian faith. This, however, was not done on a very large
scale.[9]

All of these missionary methods achieved little as far as the
conversion of the Indians was concerned. Although the number of those baptized was often large, it is doubtful that they
had a clear notion of the nature of the faith they were thereby

[8] The most notorious case, although it falls outside the scope of this
book, is that of the Jesuit missions in Paraguay, which practically disappeared when, in 1767, the Society of Jesus was expelled from all Spanish possessions.

[9] Las Casas, in F. Zubillaga, *op. cit.,* p. 243.

accepting. If the Catholic faith eventually won the allegiance of the population of the Spanish possessions in the Caribbean, this was not so much through the conversion of the original inhabitants as through their destruction and their assimilation by marriage into the Spanish population.

While the original Indian population was being subdued and destroyed, Negro slaves were being brought to the islands of the Caribbean in order to replenish the labor force.[10] Although the first Negro slaves were brought from Spain, they soon began to be imported directly from Africa. This in turn posed a new challenge to the missionary effort in the Caribbean — as well as, later, in the rest of the New World. However, the Church does not seem to have realized the importance of work among them. Seldom do we find the name of a missionary who took this task at heart. Perhaps this is partly due to the purely geographical concept of missions which was then current, and which led the friars to think of missionary work mostly in terms of going to new lands. There were, however, a few friars who did remarkable work among the Negroes, although the most noteworthy of these did not work in the Caribbean.[11] It is true that the descendants of the slaves originally brought from Africa eventually accepted the Christian faith, but this was not due so much to the missionary thrust of the Church as to the tendency of the slaves themselves to take over the customs and the faith of their masters. Even then, many rites and superstitions brought over from the ancient African cults were carried into the new faith of some of the Negroes, and often persisted until the twentieth century.

In summary, one can say that although the Spanish occupation of the Caribbean was sincerely conceived by many as a missionary enterprise, its other objectives of conquest and

---

[10] It is interesting to note that Las Casas, in his zeal to protect the Indians, suggested that Negroes be brought in to do the hard work in the fields and the mines.

[11] The two outstanding cases are Alfonso de Sandoval and Pedro Claver, both in Nueva Granada — today Colombia.

exploitation were powerful enough to mar and often destroy the missionary effort. It is true that all the islands of the Caribbean that Spain was able to retain eventually became fully Catholic, but by the time the ancient Indian rites and cults had disappeared the same was true of the Indian population as a whole. As far as Negroes were concerned, they simply adopted the Catholic faith as they slowly became reconciled to their new condition.

# III

# THE THEORY

THE SPANISH MISSIONARY ENTERPRISE INTO THE NEW WORLD gave rise to a vast production in the field of missiology. This theological activity, however, did not greatly influence the course of Christianity in the Caribbean, for the occupation of that region was complete, and the Indian population almost nonexistent, by the time when the great missiological treatises were produced. It was mostly in Peru and in territories occupied later that missiological theory really had a bearing. However, as in this first volume referring to Spanish America we are attempting to give the reader a general idea of the missionary effort of Spain at the time of the conquest of the New World, we must attempt to offer a brief summary of the beginnings of Spanish Roman Catholic missiology.[1]

---

[1] It is necessary to note that the Spanish enterprise also produced interest in missiology in other parts of Europe, as in the case of Cardinal Brancati de Laurea, who was Prefect of Studies of the Urban College of the *Propaganda*, and who in his commentary on the Third Book of Sentences of Peter Lombard included a missiological treatise. See R. Hoffman, *Pioneer Theories of Missiology, passim.*

Although the first to give some attention to the questions of missiology posed by the New World were men such as Montesinos and Las Casas, they themselves were so engaged in the active task of providing for the better treatment and conversion of the Indians that they were not able to produce anything like a systematic treatise on missions. On occasion they argued for the moral and intellectual ability of the Indians, and for the just treatment that must be given them if one expected them to become Christians. They also suggested methods of Christianization that would have been more humane than the *encomiendas*. But even so, they cannot properly be called missiologists.

The first, and no doubt the most outstanding Spanish theoretician of mission, was the Dominican professor Francisco de Vitoria, often considered to be the father of international law. The reason why he is so highly honored is to be found mainly in his two series of lectures entitled *De Indis* and *De jure belli Hispanorum in barbaros,* both delivered at Salamanca in 1539. Of these two, it is the first that has greatest bearing on the subject of missions to Spanish America. In it Francisco de Vitoria discusses the right that the kings of Spain and their subjects had to conquer the lands of the Indians. He was compelled to write on this subject by the many reports he received of atrocities committed by the *conquistadores* in the New World, especially in Peru.

The question posed in *De Indis* is whether the original inhabitants of the New World were proper masters of their private possessions, as well as of their public business; and, if so, what reasons or rights the Spanish had to dispossess them. Francisco de Vitoria's answer to the first part of the question is categorical. The Indians were in the strict sense masters and owners of their lands and other possessions. The fact that they were sinners and unbelievers did not deprive them of their right of dominion, for that right is grounded in the fact that man is made in the image of God, and there is no doubt that the same is true of the Indians. Also, one cannot argue that the Indians are not rational and thereby incapable of having possessions, for the existence of their own institutions with their own rationale proves the opposite. In conclusion, "before the Spanish arrived the Indians were true masters, both publicly and privately."[2]

As to the right that the Spanish had to conquer the New World, Vitoria set out by refuting seven false claims to such right:

> 1. That the Emperor is lord of the world. This is not true; and even if it were, the Emperor still would not have the authority to take over the lands of the "barbarians," to depose and substitute their lords, or to impose taxes.[3]
>
> 2. That the Pope has granted this right to Spain. The Pope is not the temporal lord of the whole world. His temporal power is limited to that which relates to the administration of spiritual things, and then only among Christians. Therefore the Pope has no authority over unbelievers; and if they refuse to accept his authority, that is no reason to wage war against them.
>
> 3. That Spain discovered the New World. In the strictest sense this was not true, for what Columbus "discovered" were not uninhabited lands, but territories belonging to the Indians, as has already been said.
>
> 4. That the "barbarians" refused to accept the Christian faith. This argument is false on every count. In the first place, the Indians were not committing the sin of unfaithfulness before hearing the preaching of the word. Then, they are not to be expected to believe the very first time that the faith is proclaimed to them, without any proof of its truthfulness. This includes the proof of Christians living an exemplary life, which doesn't seem to have happened too often in the New World. Finally, even if the faith had been fully and persuasively preached, taught, and proven, and the Indians refused to accept it, this would not be a sufficient reason to attack and dispossess them.
>
> 5. That the Indians were in mortal sin. If this reason were

---

[2] *De Indis*, I, 24.
[3] *Ibid.*, II, 2.

valid, and it were applied in Christian lands, kingdoms would constantly be changing from hand to hand![4]

6. That the Indians have freely chosen the lordship of the Spanish. This would only be valid had such an election taken place apart from fear and ignorance, as was clearly not the case.

7. That God has made a special grant to Spain. To this the best answer is that one should not believe those who prophesy against the common law and the teaching of Scripture, especially if their own doctrine is not confirmed by miracles.[5]

There are, however, seven valid reasons that could have been adduced for the Spanish occupation of the New World, although each can only be applied within the limits of its own conditions:

1. The Spaniards have the natural right to travel and remain in those lands, as long as they harm no one. This is to say that natural law moves man toward communication and commerce. These reasons would make it lawful for the Spanish to establish commerce with the Indians, and to expect from them all the rights that in their lands are given to foreigners. If the Indians were to refuse these rights to the Spanish, the latter would be justified in waging war against them, although always with a just sense of proportion with reference to the offense received.

2. That the Christians have the right to preach the gospel in the New World. Although properly this is the right of Christians in general, the Pope can entrust this mission to the Spanish, and preclude all others from it. If the Indians were to prohibit such preaching, the Spanish, after attempting to solve this difficulty through peaceful means, would be justified in using force against them.

3. The Spaniards would also be justified in attacking the Indians if their authorities attempted to force back into idolatry those among them who have already been converted.

4 *Ibid.*, II, 16.
5 *Ibid.*

4. If a large number of the "barbarians" have been converted, no matter by what means, the Pope can depose their princes and give them new ones, provided that there is sufficient reason for it.[6]

5. The Spanish would also be justified in attacking the Indian lords if they practiced tyranny against their subjects. Such tyranny includes human sacrifices and mass killings.

6. The Spanish would be justified in taking over the lands of the Indians if the latter, freely and truly, asked them to do so.

7. Finally, there may be cause for waging war against some of the Indians if the Spanish are led to it by alliance with others among the original inhabitants of the New World.

Apart from these seven reasons, Vitoria is inclined, although not definitely, to accept the argument of those who claim that because of the lack of intelligence of the Indians, who are like children, the lords of Spain have the right to take over their management just as a tutor takes over the management of a young child.[7]

These lectures created great unrest in Spain. Their impact was such that Charles V considered abandoning the whole overseas venture; or at least the Peruvian enterprise, which had been the direct object of Vitoria's lectures. In 1542 the Emperor promised to abandon the New World as soon as the Indians became capable of keeping themselves in the Catholic faith.[8] Many theologians became convinced that Spain was not justified in its actions in the "Indies." In Peru the debate continued for many years, and as late as 1578 we hear of a process followed by the Inquisition against Luis López, who claimed that the King of Spain did not have the right to own and rule the New World.[9]

The other great Spanish missiologist of the sixteenth century was the Jesuit father José de Acosta, a member of Vi-

---

6 *Ibid.*, II, cap. 14.

7 *Ibid.*, II, 18.

8 F. de Armas Medina, *Cristianización del Perú (1562-1600)*, p. 533.

9 *Ibid.*, p. 539.

toria's school who combined many years of academic training
with direct knowledge of missionary work among the inhabitants of the New World — especially in Peru, where he was
stationed for sixteen years. His main work is *De procuranda
Indorum salute,* published in 1588.[10]

In this work, written in six books, Acosta justifies missionary work among the Indians, but he also offers many important considerations, methodological as well as theological.

Acosta believes that the basic reason for missions is the will
of God, who does not wish that the Indians shall perish.[11]
Their purpose is the preaching of the gospel and the salvation of souls — and in this Acosta differs from many Roman
Catholic theologians of the sixteenth as well as the twentieth
centuries, who believed that the main object of missions was
the founding of the Church in new lands.[12]

Returning to the question posed by Vitoria, Acosta discusses the right that the Spanish crown has over the Indians.
Such authority is limited to those who have decided to accept
the Christian faith, and it is valid only as long as it is used for
the upbuilding of the faith, and not for its destruction.[13]
This in turn implies that not only the regular and secular
clergy, but also all the officers of the crown, and even all the
white settlers, are to be seen as joint holders of the missionary
responsibility.

Although it is impossible to determine exactly who sus-
tained such doctrines, it is clear from Acosta's opposition to
it that some entertained the idea that the Indians were incapable of receiving the Christian faith. He bases his refuta-
tion of these ideas on the common origin of all human beings,

---

10 As I have not been able to obtain a copy of the original edition,
my comments are based on the Cologne edition of 1596. There does not
seem to be a great difference between these two editions. L. Lopetegui,
"Labor misional del P. José de Acosta," *Studia Missionalia,* I (1943),
124-125.

11 *De procuranda . . . , Liber* i, cap. vi (pp. 138-144).

12 Lopetegui, *El Padre José de Acosta . . . ,* pp. 264-272.

13 *Ibid.,* p. 251.

as found in the book of Genesis, and on the abundant texts of Scripture that promise salvation to the Gentiles. However, he believes that the Indians are inferior to the Spaniards, and that they should not be allowed to enter the ranks of the clergy.[14]

What are the Indians required to believe in order to be saved? At the time when Acosta was writing his *De procuranda,* the Dominican Francisco de la Cruz was claiming that the Indians should only be expected to believe in a just and judging God, and in the divine origin of the Christian faith. Acosta cannot accept this notion that it is possible to preach the gospel without including in it the knowledge of Christ. This implies a certain acceptance of the doctrine of the Trinity, no matter how elementary. Also, the Indians must understand the nature of the Church, not as a Spanish organization, but as a divine and an infallible institution. These requirements are the main reason why Acosta condemned the common practice of baptizing Indians and Negro slaves who hardly had an idea of the nature of the Christian faith.

Besides these fundamental points of doctrine, Acosta discusses many other very important practical aspects of the missionary enterprise, such as the administration of the sacrament of marriage, the studies and moral character to be expected of the missionaries, and others. But these would take us far beyond the scope of this book.

After Vitoria and Acosta, Roman Catholic missiology flourished in the person of Tomás de Jesús, who in 1613 published his work *De procuranda salute omnium gentium.* From then on, missiology was no longer a particular concern of Spanish and Portuguese theologians, but rather a part of Roman Catholic theology in Europe.

---

[14] *De procuranda...*, *Liber* vi, cap. xix (pp. 565-567).

# IV

# THE ESTABLISHMENT OF THE
# HIERARCHY AND FURTHER
# DEVELOPMENT

THE FIRST SPANISH SETTLEMENT IN THE NEW WORLD WAS FORT
Natividad, on the island Columbus named Hispaniola — little
Spain. Today that island is uneasily shared by Haiti and the
Dominican Republic, pointing to a complex history of rivalry
between the Spanish and French colonial powers. This chapter, however, deals with the history of the Church under the
Spanish regime, and it will thus be necessary in other chapters to deal with the Church under the French regime, and
with the development of Christianity after Dominican independence.

On the other hand, this chapter will include brief sections
on Puerto Rico and Cuba under the flag of Spain, and later
chapters will deal with independent Cuba and with Puerto
Rico under the American flag.

In Hispaniola the first Spanish settlement was short lived.
The Spaniards Columbus left behind exploited the Indians

to such a point that they rebelled, and when the Admiral returned on his second voyage he found only the charred remains of what he had hoped would be the beginning of further colonization.

Columbus, however, would not give up his plans of colonization. After seeking a more propitious emplacement, he founded a new settlement. But the rivalries among the Spaniards were such, and the discontent so great, that Columbus was recalled to Spain, and taken back in chains. Meanwhile, he and his fellow adventurers had created such ill will among the Indians that it was very difficult to gain true converts.

The first missionaries to Hispaniola did not contribute greatly to change this situation. Their leader, Father Boyl, became disenchanted and decided to return to Spain. Some of the others remained, but most of them trusted more in the sword of the Spaniards than in the power of the gospel to gain converts.

In spite of all this the "Christianization" of the island marched forward, mostly through the elimination and assimilation of the Indian population. Many of the Indians, not accustomed to heavy work, committed suicide rather than subject to the toils imposed on them by their *encomenderos*. Others died due to diseases brought by the Spaniards and against which they had no resistance. Many women were forcibly taken by the Spaniards — who usually took the precaution of avoiding mortal sin by having the Indian women baptized before taking them — thereby reducing the pure Indian population and giving rise to a large number of "mestizos" who would eventually be looked down upon by the Spaniards themselves. Finally, the Indians who remained either took to the hills or received baptism as a way to survive in what had suddenly become a foreign land.

This does not mean that there were no able missionaries among the Spanish priests. The Hieronymite Román Pane learned several Indian dialects, and studied their customs and religion in sufficient depth to be able to present Christianity to them in a reasonable light. The Mercedarian Juan Infante went into the purely Indian country and was rewarded by the sincere conversion of some families.[1] But, by and large, the shadow cast by the Spaniards in general was such that it was very difficult, even for the best and most zealous missionaries, to approach the Indians with the word of the cross.

Meanwhile the Spanish settlements were growing. This led to the permanent establishment of monastic houses and to the organization of an ecclesiastical hierarchy. The first Franciscan house was founded in 1502; and the first Dominican, in 1509. This Dominican monastery was under the direction of Pedro de Córdoba, one of the most zealous missionaries in Hispaniola.[2] These monasteries served the Church in two ways: as centers of education for the youth — although mostly the Spanish youth — and as sources of missionaries to the new settlements and even beyond.

The missionaries as well as the secular authorities advocated the establishment of a hierarchy. In 1504 Pope Julius II erected three episcopal sees in Hispaniola. The sees were never occupied, however, and the opposition of the Spanish crown to some of the procedures of the Pope led to their suppression. Later, in August of 1511, Julius II, after due negotiation with Spain, erected three sees, of which two were in Hispaniola — Santo Domingo and Concepción de la Vega, and one in Puerto Rico — San Juan.[3] These three sees were placed under the jurisdiction of the archdiocese of Seville. In this the ecclesiastical authorities were merely reflecting the practice established by the crown, whereby all commerce with the "Indies" had to take place through the port of Seville. After this time the religious condition of the island improved until the beginning of the seventeenth century, when it decayed again.

The often repeated notion that the Catholic Church in Latin America did not take at heart the education of the faithful is a myth. It may well be true that at a later date,

---

1 F. Zubillaga in *Historia de la Iglesia...*, p. 221.

2 J. Verschueren, *La République d'Haïti*, I, 190.

3 Zubillaga in *Historia de la Iglesia...*, p. 248.

when the first missionary zeal was spent, and when Spain itself was going through evil times, the Church concentrated its attention on the education of the clergy and of the higher strata of society. But the eagerness of some of the early missionaries and prelates to offer higher education, not only to the Spaniards, but also to the natives, is remarkable. Through the offices of the Dominican missionaries Pope Paul III authorized the founding of the Dominican University of Saint Thomas, and granted its graduates and degrees full equality with those of the old country. This was done in 1538, only twenty-nine years after the establishment of the first Dominican monastery, and quite a few years before the chartering of the first English-speaking universities in the New World. It is also important to point out that from the very beginning of negotiations for its establishment, this university aspired to be a center of higher education for Indians as well as Spaniards. Unfortunately, this institution later suffered some setbacks due to the fact that the Dominican missionaries who requested its establishment did so by writing directly to Rome, and that therefore the crown felt that it had been slighted.[4]

Another institution of higher learning was founded in 1558, through a royal decree granted after almost thirty years of repeated petitions from the hierarchy and the civil authorities of Santo Domingo. This university also stated clearly its purpose to educate the Indians as well as the whites, and as far as can be known it did so until the Indian population disappeared.

The most remarkable bishop of Santo Domingo was don Alonso de Fuenmayor (1539-1554), who in 1545 had his see elevated to the rank of archdiocese, with jurisdiction over all other sees in the Indies.[5] Besides giving full support to higher learning for men, he provided for the education of girls. A remarkable builder, he supervised the construction of several

---

[4] *Ibid.*, pp. 476-477.
[5] Verschueren, *La République* ... , p. 191.

ecclesiastical edifices, and also directed the building and arming of the walls and fortifications of the city.[6]

At the end of the sixteenth century the archdiocese of Santo Domingo had nineteen parishes, almost all of enormous extension, but which practically covered the island.[7]

The seventeenth century was a period of decline in Hispaniola as well as in the other Spanish colonies in the Caribbean. The discovery and conquest of new and richer lands — notably Mexico and Peru — depleted the population of the older colonies. The marked decrease in the Indian population made it necessary to rely on Negro slaves, and these were costly. Pirates harassed the coasts, and many of the settlers, in an effort to break the stiff monopoly of Seville, traded with them. In consequence, the king resolved to transfer inland several of the settlements on the northern coast, and this in turn brought greater confusion and decay. The most able missionaries were claimed by the vast territories of Mexico and Peru, and therefore the clergy in Santo Domingo was composed mostly of those who were not able to perform the priestly functions in Spain and lacked the zeal and courage to go to the new territories. We are told that in 1650 the total population consisted of twelve thousand Spaniards and five thousand Negroes. There were about forty priests, of whom eighteen were attached to the cathedral — thereby leaving about twenty for all the rest of the colony. Of these only one — a mulatto — could be described as "a man of letters."[8]

The Jesuits came to the island in 1650, in an attempt to remedy the situation. Their numbers, however, were so few that there was very little they could do. The first two missionaries contracted some form of tropical illness and died. Their most notable member, who distinguished himself through his work among the Negroes, was not a Spaniard, but an Italian — his true name was Molinelli, although he hispanicized it to "Molina." Finally, after 1660, the number and work of the

---

6 Zubillaga, *Historia de la Iglesia* ..., p. 479.

7 *Ibid.*, p. 480.

8 *Ibid.*, pp. 779-785.

Jesuits increased, and this brought a notable improvement to the spiritual life of the colony.[9]

The most able churchman of this period was the Dominican archbishop of Santo Domingo, Domingo Fernández Navarrete (1677-1685). Besides being an able administrator and a conscientious pastor, he helped the island recover from the disastrous earthquake of 1684.[10]

However, neither the Jesuits nor a few able archbishops were able to check the decline of the colony and of its ecclesiastical life. Earlier in the century the French had taken possession of the small island of Tortuga, off the western coast of Hispaniola. From Tortuga they moved onto the larger island, and their eastward expansion became a direct threat to the Spanish settlements, which were concentrated in the East. In the next century, when there was a small degree of reconstruction, a brutal earthquake (1751) destroyed most of the capital, and the next year a hurricane destroyed a great deal of what was still standing. In 1767, Charles III ordered the expulsion of all Jesuits from his lands, and this was a further blow to the precarious Church that had been established in Hispaniola.

Finally, as an indirect consequence of the French Revolution, the whole island was turned over to France, and the Spanish there were forced to live under a foreign yoke. In the French sector of Hispaniola the echoes of the French Revolution produced a rebellion of the Negro population, claiming for themselves the freedom and equality that the French proclaimed elsewhere. Oddly enough, in order to support Spain in its war against France, the inhabitants of Santo Domingo supported this rebellion, and were thus involved in a long struggle in which they usually had the upper hand. However, when the time came to settle the conflict, Spain was naturally more interested in preserving her geographic integrity than in the distant colony of Hispaniola, and therefore traded the

---

9 *Ibid.*, pp. 785-788.
10 *Ibid.*, pp. 789-794.

latter in exchange for the Spanish cities held by the French. Thus (1795), the pro-Spanish and conservative settlers in Hispaniola found themselves abandoned to the authority of the revolutionary French, whom they had learned to hate through years of bitter struggle. This increased their hatred for the French oppressors, and it also gave rise to a nationalistic feeling that the hispanic population of the island could no longer trust Spain as their mother country.

Later on we shall see how Christianity fared under the French (Ch. V), as well as under the two independent countries of Haiti (Ch. VI) and the Dominican Republic (Ch. VII). Now, however, we must turn to the history of Christianity under the Spanish regime in Puerto Rico and Cuba.

During his second voyage, while en route to Fort Natividad in Hispaniola, Columbus discovered an island that he named San Juan Bautista. Later on a city was founded on that island and christened Puerto Rico — "rich port." Even later on, by an odd interchange of names, the island came to be known as Puerto Rico, and the city became San Juan. It is therefore anachronistic to refer to Columbus' discovery of Puerto Rico, or to the founding of San Juan. However, for the sake of clarity and consistency, we shall take upon ourselves the burden of that anachronism, and refer to both the island and the city by their actual names.

As has been said above, the diocese of San Juan was erected in 1511. This is quite remarkable, for it was scarcely three years before that don Juan Ponce de León had begun the permanent colonization of the island. If one takes into consideration the tardiness of communications at that time, and the need for negotiations between Spain and Rome, it follows that the diocese was erected practically with no real certainty as to what would be the results of the plan of colonization.

The first bishop of San Juan was don Alonso Manso (1512-1534), a man of ample culture who created a school of grammar where the clergy were able to improve their training. Although still revered in Puerto Rico as its first bishop and founder of its first school, Bishop Manso seems to have spent a great deal of time away from his diocese, mostly in Spain.

Even more than Hispaniola, Puerto Rico became a mere stopping place for further conquest. Ponce de León himself, after a relatively short stay on the island, left it in pursuit of the Fountain of Youth. As in the case of Hispaniola, the opening of Mexico and Peru depleted the population of the island, as well as its clergy. By the second half of the fifteenth century, the bishop had only ten or twelve priests, and there was only one monastery on the island.[11]

The treatment of the Indians was somewhat better than in Hispaniola, for the crown was now more aware of the abuses to which they could be subjected, and took steps to curb them.

In several instances small groups of Indians were given their freedom back after having been "Christianized," on condition that they were to live in places accessible to the missionaries. Eventually, as in all the Spanish colonies of the Caribbean, the Indian population was partially destroyed and partially absorbed, so that there no longer was a need for missions among them.

The conditions of poverty and depopulation of the sixteenth century prevailed also through the seventeenth, and even into the first two or three decades of the eighteenth. However, Puerto Rico was becoming increasingly important for the Spanish crown, for it was a key point in the route to be followed by the gold from Mexico and Peru. Therefore the Spanish authorities took steps to populate and fortify the island against possible attacks. One such step was the use of part of the gold from Mexico for the construction of walls, fortresses, and storehouses. Another such step was garrisoning the port with troops from Spain. The net result of all this was that early in the eighteenth century the population began to grow again, and by the end of the century there were about 150,000 inhabitants.[12]

---

11 *Ibid.*, p. 483.
12 *Ibid.*, p. 808.

Meanwhile the Church had not ceased having difficulties. When the population was scarce and most poor, the bishops repeatedly reported that they did not have the necessary resources, both human and financial. Late in the seventeenth century Bishop Padilla requested from Spain that some monies owed him be paid in textiles, for the people were so poor that they were ashamed to send their almost naked children to school. Just a few months later a smallpox epidemic killed twenty-one out of the twenty-five priests on the island (1690).

Later, when conditions began improving, the Church was not able to cope with the rising population, and again we hear of bishops complaining that they have very few priests, and that even these are almost illiterate.

It was toward the end of the eighteenth century that the Church once again took a position of leadership in founding schools and building and improving hospitals. In the religious field the eighteenth century also saw some improvement with an increase in the number of clergy (and probably in their education), the growth of the very few convents, and the reconstruction of old and dilapidated churches. Most remarkable in this new upsurge of church life was Bishop Juan Bautista Zengotita Bengoa (1794-1802), who not only visited his clergy and requested funds from Spain for building hospitals and churches, but also used his private funds for many works of charity and for the defense of the island against the British.

The nineteenth century was the period of the great wars of independence in Spanish America. These wars brought to Puerto Rico a large number of exiles — mainly from Venezuela — who were loyal to Spain. As there were priests among these exiles, the number of clergy grew. Puerto Rico became an important military base for the pursuit of war, and therefore the Spanish government paid more attention to this small colony which was to be — together with Cuba — its last holding in the New World. This did not necessarily mean a policy granting greater freedom, but it did mean greater revenues and more competent manpower. The net result for the Church was a period of over half a century in which there was a fair number of priests, almost adequate financial resources, and a deeper religious life than had been the case.

The second half of the century brought tension between the Puerto Ricans and Spain. Although Puerto Rico was still mostly faithful to Spain, and not usually aiming at independence, the sentiment grew that it should have a greater degree of autonomy, and that Puerto Ricans, rather than Spaniards, should rule their own island. At the same time, mostly through contacts with the ideas of the French and the American Revolutions, a liberal movement was developing. In 1870, during the Republican regime in Spain, permission was granted for the establishment of a Protestant school in the offshore island of Vieques. In 1873, following a decree in Spain granting religious tolerance, an Anglican church was founded in the southern city of Ponce. Although these liberal concessions were very much restricted with the reestablishment of the Spanish monarchy, the autonomist movement continued to grow, and in 1897 autonomy was finally granted to the island. It was too late, for in 1898 the Spanish-American War would change the destinies of Puerto Rico.

By and large the Catholic hierarchy, being composed of native Spaniards, showed little sympathy for the autonomist cause. Although some of the lower clergy were in favor of it, this did not destroy the bad feeling toward the hierarchy that developed as a consequence of the bishops' attitude. This contributed to weaken a Church that had never been strong.

Under the American regime that Church would have to undergo a process of deep and painful change.

Ever since he discovered it in his first voyage, Columbus was greatly interested in Cuba, which he took to be part of the Asiatic mainland. He himself later attempted to circumnavigate the island and failed. It was in 1508 that Sebastián de Ocampo, by sailing around Cuba, proved that it was an island. In 1511 don Diego Velázquez sailed from Hispaniola with about three hundred men, with the purpose of conquering and colonizing the island. Among his company were several men who were later to become famous: Hernán Cortés, Pedro de Alvarado, Bernal Díaz del Castillo, and, later, Pánfilo de Narváez. After founding Baracoa in the western tip of the island, the *conquistadores* split into three columns and marched westward, subduing the Indians, collecting gold, and founding towns — Bayamo in 1513, Trinidad, Sancti-Spiritus, and Santiago de Cuba in 1514, and Puerto Príncipe and San Cristóbal de La Habana in 1515.[13] Except for a brief and hopeless attempt under the leadership of Hatuey, an Indian chief from Hispaniola who had come to Cuba fleeing the Spaniards,[14] there was no resistance on the part of the Indians, who were peaceful and primitive people — especially in the West. This did not prevent all sorts of cruelties against them, and even mass killings, such as that which took place in Caonao, where the Spaniards tricked the Indians into a feast and then killed them with no reason whatsoever, except greed for their scarce gold and their women.

Even before Velázquez conquered the island, some zealous Franciscans had visited it with missionary purposes, but had achieved no results. During Velázquez's campaign, and always from then on, the first and central building in every town was the church. The first Cuban diocese was erected in Baracoa in 1517, and transferred in 1522 to the more important Santiago de Cuba. A few years later a Franciscan monastery was founded in Santiago, with the hope that it would become a center of missionary work to the neighboring regions.

In spite of this seemingly complete organization, the state of the Church was very poor, spiritually even more than ma-

---

13 Only one of these towns, Puerto Príncipe, was on the northern coast. Havana was on the southern coast and was later moved twice before it came to where it now stands. Puerto Príncipe was later moved inland, and thus Havana became the main city on the northern coast. Still, Santiago de Cuba, on the southern coast, was for several years the capital city of the colony.

14 It is said that when Hatuey was captured and tied to the stake he was asked if he wanted to become a Christian and thus go to heaven. Hatuey asked whether the Spaniards went to heaven. Upon being told that it was so, he responded that he would rather not go to such a place.

terially, and remained so for a long time. The first bishop, Juan de Ubite, was able to organize the chapter of his cathedral, and even to open a school, but he resigned after a few years, convinced of the futility of his efforts. His successor, Miguel Ramírez, was an ambitious man who used his office to enrich himself and to crush those who opposed him. In connivance with Governor Gonzalo de Guzmán, he arranged things so that most of the lands and of the Indians were allotted to him, to the governor, or to their supporters. When a local judge opposed him, he invoked inquisitorial powers — which he did not have — and excommunicated the judge. He opposed the founding of the Franciscan monastery in Santiago, mostly because he feared that its inmates would agitate against the *encomiendas* and against his dishonest dealings. Finally both he and the governor were recalled to Spain in disgrace (1532).[15]

His successor, Diego Sarmiento, was an honest man, but was unable to cope with the disheartening conditions that he found upon his arrival at the island. These conditions had to do mostly with a great shortage of manpower and with the very poor quality of that which was available. Only in Santiago and Bayamo were there more than one priest. Santiago was the city with by far the largest provision of clergy, there being three priests serving at the cathedral and a few Franciscans at the monastery. The spiritual level at the monastery was deplorable, there having been cases of dishonesty and of crass ineptitude. A few of the monks, however, had done some missionary work in the eastern part of the island — and this was one of the very few bright spots in the bishop's report to the crown. In all other towns the ministry of the Church was limited to the local residents, usually a few Spaniards and larger contingents of local Indians given in *encomienda,* of Negro slaves, and of Indian slaves brought in from Yucatán. The bishop himself, convinced as Ubite had been of the futility of his task, simply returned to Spain.[16]

---

[15] Zubillaga, in *Historia de la Iglesia ...,* pp. 279-281.
[16] *Ibid.,* pp. 281-284.

The second half of the century brought even further decay, except perhaps, and only in some aspects, to Havana.[17] Gold was becoming ever more scarce in the rivers, and new lands — Mexico, Peru, and Florida — offered new riches. Most of the Indian population had disappeared — only about five thousand were left — and it was necessary for the whites either to buy expensive Negro slaves or to stoop to manual labor — which they would not. Pirates and corsairs ravaged the coasts. The moral and spiritual condition of the island declined further due to an ecclesiastical reform in Spain, which set the most unworthy priests to sailing to the New World. As Havana was a forced stop for most of these priests, their immoral deeds shattered the moral fiber of the city.[18]

The seventeenth century was even worse than the sixteenth. Early in the century Santiago was no more than fifteen or sixteen straw houses, and in Havana there was not even a church.[19] The French based in Tortuga, and the British in Jamaica, continually attacked the Cuban coasts. Priests were more scarce than ever, and the moral life of the people seems to have been at its all-time low.

Conditions began improving in the eighteenth century, when the Jesuits settled in Havana (1724) and later in Puerto Príncipe (1751). In Havana they opened a school that eventually became a theological seminary. This respite, however, was short lived, for in 1767 the Jesuits were expelled from all Spanish territories.

Two other sources of improvement were the taking of Havana by the British and the liberal government of Charles III of Spain. When the British took Havana, they allowed ships

---

17 Having become an important link between Mexico, Peru, and Florida on the one hand, and Spain on the other, Havana profited from increased commerce, and its population grew through the establishment of a garrison brought mostly from Mexico.

18 That this is no exaggeration can better be understood by pointing out that at times these wandering priests totaled almost a hundred. Zubillaga, *Historia de la Iglesia . . .* , pp. 474-475.

19 *Ibid.*, p. 768.

from different nationalities to come into the port and to trade with the city. This broke the traditional Spanish monopoly, improved the finances of the city, and opened the way for new and revolutionary ideas from Europe. When the British left Havana, Spain could not simply revert to the old monopolistic practices, and a decree of 1769 allowed the city freer trade, which in turn brought in the news and ideas of the French and American Revolutions. This trend was reinforced by the various edicts of Charles III granting greater liberties to the colonies. Ecclesiastically this resulted in priests with a better education, and in a greater number of them. By the end of the century Cuba was undoubtedly entering a period of solid religious and cultural life.[20] The problems that the Church now faced were not so much those of poverty, but those of excessive riches, which affected the purity of monastic life and the pastoral work of more than one priest and bishop. The other problem confronting the Church was how to maintain its authority in the face of the invasion of liberal and even revolutionary ideas.[21]

During the first half of the nineteenth century the new conditions resulted in remarkable improvement in Church life and leadership. In 1802 the see of Havana was occupied by the man who was its most remarkable bishop: Juan José Díaz de Espada y Landa. During the thirty years of his reign he reformed the clergy, widened the studies at San Carlos Seminary, founded new parishes, built cemeteries, gave great impulse to learning, and even became the chief promoter of vaccination.[22] Under his leadership the Church ceased to be a

---

20 By the end of the century there were a flourishing university, several institutions of theological education, and a great number of schools.

21 The most important importer of these ideas was the *Real Sociedad Económica de Amigos del País,* founded in 1792.

22 Although Dr. Tomás Romay was the main advocate for vaccination in Havana, Bishop Espada contributed by enrolling his clergy in a campaign to vaccinate those who lived in the country. When doctors were not available, Espada's clergy would vaccinate the population. In a few years smallpox had ceased to be the threat it had always been.

conservative institution and became the leader of Cuban intellectual life.

This renaissance, however, was short lived. The second half of the century brought new difficulties to the Catholic Church. The new ideas that were connected with the French and American revolutions were taking root among the people. As the native Spaniards looked upon the Cubans with contempt, these ideas were mingled with a growing sense of nationality. After the middle of the century, conspiracies against Spain became more and more common. In 1868, rebellion broke out, and lasted until 1878 — the Ten Years' War. Although conditions were never completely peaceful after that, open warfare began again in 1895. This time it spread throughout the Island. In response, the Spanish authorities took harsh measures that decimated the civilian population. In 1898, when the Island was aflame with rebellion, the United States declared war on Spain and quickly defeated it. After four years of American government, Cuba became independent in 1902. During all these struggles, the vast majority of the clergy remained faithful to Spain. Not only were they themselves Spaniards, but the Pope himself had granted to Spain sovereignty over Cuba, so that opposition to such sovereignty was very near to heresy. Therefore, all of the higher clergy, and most of the lower, opposed Cuban independence. The few priests who dared speak a word, not even for independence, but simply for more liberal conditions, were suspected and even excommunicated. Often clergy learned of conspiracies at the confessional, and they hastened to warn the authorities and give them details and even names of the persons involved. In consequence, the Church — and specially the clergy — lost most of its prestige. Patriots would chide the Church and meet in clandestine Masonic lodges in order to conspire. Excommunication became a mark of worth and intellectual freedom. Yet this did not lead most of these men to renounce Christianity or even Catholicism. They were convinced Christians, and, as most of them knew no other form of Christianity, they remained Catholics, although at the same time they despised the clergy and the Spanish government that lurked behind it. Thus developed a strong anticlerical, but not anti-Catholic feeling which would persist at least into the second half of the twentieth century, and which in part explains why the Church as an organization proved so weak at the time of Castro's revolution. That story, however, belongs in a later chapter.

# V

# THE COMING OF THE FRENCH

As has already been said, around 1630 the French established a small settlement at Tortuga. This was not an official French colony, but rather a center for the activities of filibusters who sailed from Tortuga, captured small prizes, and returned to their base in order to replenish their stores and dispose of their booty. The settlement, however, was viewed with sympathy by the French crown, for it harassed Spanish colonies and also provided for a measure of commerce between France and the Caribbean. Thus, by the second half of the century France was ready to appoint the first official governor, Bertrand d'Ogeron. Meanwhile the French settlers had moved into the western section of Hispaniola and had expanded their activities, which now included agriculture and some commerce with the filibusters as well as with France.

Naturally, Spain opposed this intrusion in what it deemed its territories. Although the western part of Hispaniola had never been colonized by the Spaniards, the Pope had granted to them this land, and the French were clearly intruders in foreign property. Thus fighting between the French and the Spanish was almost continuous, and did not cease even after Spain had officially acknowledged French sovereignty over the western section of the Island — in the Treaty of Ryswick, 1697.

As the Indians had called this western section of Hispaniola Haiti, that name prevailed, although one often finds the French themselves referring to the Island as Saint-Domingue — the later Spanish name.

The French colony of Haiti was seemingly very prosperous. Although gold was not abundant, the land was fertile, and soon there were great plantations of sugar cane and cacao. As sugar and chocolate commanded very high prices in Europe, the colonists grew rich and developed a life of comfort and luxury that even led some chroniclers to compare Port-au-Prince with Paris. This prosperity, however, was based on very large numbers of slaves, and on the subjection and exploitation of the free Negroes and the mulatto population. In 1789 there were 520,000 inhabitants in Haiti. Of these, 452,000 were slaves, 28,000 freedmen and only 40,000 white.[1] This created a very tense situation, which would explode when the fires of the French Revolution reached Haiti.

As was to be expected due to the character and occupation of its original population, the French colony of Haiti did not enjoy a very deep religious life during its first years. Furthermore, the hierarchical structure of the Church took a long time to be established, first due to the extra-official nature of the colony, and later due to the troubles brought about by the Negro revolt.

During the seventeenth century there was no hierarchical structure whatsoever in the Catholic Church in Haiti. In 1640 there were thirteen churches and eight priests to serve six thousand inhabitants scattered over a wide area.[2] By this time, however, France was beginning to pay more attention

---

[1] J. Verschueren, *Panorama d'Haïti*, I, 52.
[2] *Ibid.*, pp. 191-192.

to the nascent colony, and in consequence there was to be a greater influx of colonists as well as priests. It was thus that the French Dominicans entered the Island in 1684, and the Jesuits in 1704 — a year earlier, however, the Capuchins had abandoned their mission. In 1705 the French section of the Island was divided in two apostolic prefectures. The *Préfecture du Nord* was placed under the care of the Jesuits, and the *Préfecture du Sud* under that of the Dominicans.[3]

The work of the Dominicans was not easy. Their numbers were always small, not so much because they lacked recruits from France, but because the climate and the hardships of constant and difficult travel continually decimated them. Just before the establishment of the *Préfecture du Sud,* and in a period of ten years, twenty-six Dominicans had perished, and a number had felt forced to return to France. If one considers the fact that during those years there were usually less than a dozen Dominicans in Haiti, one sees that the toll was high and the life expectancy of a missionary very short indeed.[4] In spite of this the Dominicans continued their work, not only among the whites, but also among the increasing Negro population. This was even more difficult, for to the hardships of climate and health were added the negative attitudes of the white colonists, most of whom felt that if the Negroes were kept in ignorance it would be easier to keep them in subjection. Thus, due to the scarcity of missionaries and to the lack of cooperation of the white colonists, the Christianization of the Negroes was very superficial. This resulted in the survival of ancient African beliefs and rites, mixed with Christian elements in what is termed Voodoo.[5]

In spite of these difficulties, the history of the Dominican mission in Haiti is one of devotion, sacrifice, and even some-

---

3 *Ibid.,* p. 192.

4 *Ibid.,* p. 194.

5 As Voodoo is an important aspect of Haitian religious life, we shall discuss it in this book. However, as most serious studies of it are concerned with its most recent manifestations, we shall discuss it in the chapter that deals with Haiti after its independence.

times of learning and enlightenment. Father Nicolson, for instance, composed the first treatise on Haitian botany.

At the *Préfecture du Nord,* the Jesuits did not fare much better than the Dominicans. Although not quite as great as that of the Dominicans, their mortality rate was also astounding. They encountered the same difficulties of climate, and the attitude of their white constituency was not always respectful, and almost always suspicious, of their work among the Negroes. Therefore, they too were unable to bring the Negro population to a deep understanding and acceptance of the Christian faith, and Voodoo remained as prevalent in the *Préfecture du Nord* as it was in the South.

Father Le Pers arrived at Haiti with the first contingent of Jesuit missionaries. His passion was for founding new parishes, so that the services of the Church could reach more directly and deeply into the countryside. He was especially interested in work among the Negroes, and did all he could to help them understand the nature of the Christian faith. Besides, he occupied his free time in collecting data regarding the history and the flora of Haiti, so that two of the first books in these fields, although not published by him, were based on his research.[6]

Father Boutin arrived at Haiti a year after Le Pers. After having served in two other parishes, he was transferred to Ville du Cap, where most of his apostolic labors took place. There he began his work by leading his parishioners in building a new church, for the old wooden one was not in good condition. Then he began building a hospital for the poor, but having received the promise from another order that they would admit the poor in their hospital, he turned his building into an orphanage for girls. This institution, however, met with the opposition of the civil and ecclesiastical authorities, and he therefore transformed it into a

---

[6] Charlevoix, *Histoire de Saint-Domingue* (1730) and Desportes, *Maladies de Saint-Domingue* (1770), which takes from Le Pers its knowledge of medicinal herbs (Verschueren, *op. cit.,* II, 235-236).

school for girls. These administrative and building interests were not sufficient to demand all the energies of Father Boutin, who also devoted a great deal of time to minister to the sailors who came into port, and especially to the Negroes.

Father Boutin's work among the Negroes was the most commendable aspect of his career. He loved and respected th .m enough to learn several of their African dialects, so that he was able to communicate even with those who had arrived from Africa most recently. His constant care for the Negroes caused him to be loved by them, and at the same time made him suspect by the white authorities. He founded the "Negroes' Mass," which took place on Sundays, after the regular mass, and in which the catechism was taught to the Negroes in such a way that they could understand it.

The measure of this man is perhaps the fact that, in spite of all his responsibilities and tasks, he found time to make acute astronomical observations. When he died in 1742, even his opponents had to acknowledge that he was a man of great sanctity and firm resolution.[7]

Even the slight progress made by Dominicans and Jesuits was to be shattered late in the eighteenth century, when the echoes of the French Revolution gave rise in Haiti to waves of revolt and terror much greater than those which France ever knew.[8] In 1790 the French revolutionary government decreed full civil rights for all freedmen. The local authorities, under the pressure of the white colonists, refused to obey the decree. Seeing this, the mulatto and black freedmen revolted under the leadership of Ogé and Chavannes. After a few early victories, the rebels were defeated and mass executions and other terrors followed. This, however, simply served to increase the bitterness of the freedmen, who continued to revolt under their new chief, the mulatto Beauvais.

Meanwhile, the slaves, encouraged by the freedman revolt,

---

[7] *Ibid.*, II, 237-239.
[8] A story very well told in *ibid.*, pp. 24-50.

also became restless. A Voodoo priest named Boukman incited and led them to rebellion. This time the cruelties were unspeakable. Great numbers of white colonists were killed in the most terrible ways that their former slaves could devise, and their plantations and homes were put to the torch. The rebellion, which had begun in the North, soon covered the whole of Haiti, and only in the larger towns, under the protection of their garrisons, could the whites find any measure of safety.

Conditions became even more chaotic through the intervention of foreign powers. Oddly enough, Spain proclaimed herself the champion of the Negroes' cause, and under that guise invaded Haiti from the East. The British took the cause of the white settlers against the freedmen and against the French authorities, which now were inclined to grant the freedmen their full civil rights. Thus several seaports were occupied by the British.

In the midst of this chaos, faced with the possibility of entirely losing the colony, the French played their last and desperate card: they proclaimed the freedom of all slaves. This changed the situation completely, for the blacks now turned to defending Haiti against the Spanish and British invaders as well as fighting the white colonists, and the latter were placed in the untenable position of fighting for the British and against their own country, France. In this struggle two native leaders gained prominence: the mulatto Rigaud in the South, and the Negro ex-slave Toussaint Louverture in the North. They repeatedly defeated the enemy. Spain, conquered not only in Hispaniola, but also in Europe, signed a treaty in 1795 by which it recognized French sovereignty, not just over Haiti, but over all the island of Hispaniola. Finally, in 1798, Toussaint defeated the last British forces on the Island. For these services the French government made him a general and commander-in-chief of the troops in the colony. After that he was practically master of the Island. The French authorities tried to undermine his power by giving prominence to Rigaud, and civil war was the consequence, with further killings and the flight of over two thousand white colonists. Finally, Toussaint overcame Rigaud and remained effective master of the Island for years, for although France continued to appoint governors, it was Toussaint who told them what to do and who sent them home if they did not act according to his wishes. In 1801 a constitution was approved that made Haiti practically autonomous, and Toussaint became Governor for life, with the right to name his own successor.

Napoleon, however, could not tolerate such an attitude even in a distant colony. Having practically conquered Europe, he felt that he could spare the resources to bring Haiti to submission — for although Toussaint had not proclaimed the independence of the colony, it was clear that he took himself to be the true and only government of the Island, and that the colored Haitians — by now almost all the population that was left in the Island — were more loyal to him and to their newly acquired freedom than to Napoleon or France. Therefore the French Consul sent a mighty army under the command of his brother-in-law, General Leclerc. After a long and costly campaign Leclerc defeated Toussaint, who was finally captured through a dishonorable ruse. Taken to France and imprisoned there, the Negro leader died in less than a year.

The capture of Toussaint did not kill all opposition to Leclerc and his army, and the French general resorted to terror in order to make the Haitians submit. This in turn led once more to open rebellion, which now took the form of guerrilla warfare. Under the leadership of Dessalines the Haitians became aware that they were fighting for national independence. In 1803 a flag was created. Decimated by yellow fever, the French surrendered in November of that same year, and the first of January of 1804 Dessalines proclaimed the independence of Haiti.

All of this fighting, especially when it took the form of disorderly revolt or of oppressive terror, resulted in the destruction of a great portion of the Island's riches, as well as in

cruelties and massacres that would not be forgotten for gen-
erations. Most of the white population fled, and with them
went a great deal of technical and administrative skill. Many
of the former slaves, who used to equate slavery with work,
refused to contribute to the general welfare. Others among
the new leaders conducted themselves in the same fashion in
which their white masters had previously done. All of this resulted in evil times for the country as well as for the Church.

As far as the Church is concerned, one should note that
more often than not priests were spared in the midst of mass
killings of whites. This shows that in spite of all difficulties
they had somehow succeeded in gaining the good will of the
slaves. Many churches, however, were destroyed and sacked.
Often the cause of Negro freedom was furthered in the name
of the ancient African gods of Voodoo, although in other
cases Negro leaders, such as Toussaint Louverture, forbade
the practice of Voodoo, which they considered detrimental to
the national character.

In any case the years of revolt brought great difficulties to
the Catholic Church, for priests were ever more scarce, church
buildings were mostly in ruins, and the general atmosphere
tended to draw attention away from religion and toward
moral and physical excesses.

When independence was proclaimed, the Church was at a
low ebb, and it had a formidable task before it. That story,
however, belongs in our next chapter.

# PART TWO

# CHRISTIANITY UNDER
THE NEW REGIMES

# VI

# HAITI

AFTER HAITIAN INDEPENDENCE, CHRISTIANITY THERE HAS EXISTED over against a background of instability, poverty, and Voodooism.

Politically,[1] it is clear that the Haitians, who fought valiantly and even sometimes gallantly to gain their independence, were not ready to govern themselves. General Dessalines, the leader of the movement for independence, had himself proclaimed Governor for life, and later on, imitating Napoleon, took the title of Emperor. His reign was noted for its cruelty and bad management. One of his first orders upon becoming Governor was to have all whites killed, except priests and doctors. Later on, due to his mismanagement, the public treasury went bankrupt. He met his death in an ambush at the hands of a group of his former followers.

Emperor Dessalines was followed in the North by President Christophe, and in the South by President Pétion. Thus the

[1] The political history of Haiti is ably and briefly told in Verschueren, *Panorama d'Haïti*, I, 57-77, and II, 51-178.

country was divided from 1807 to 1820. Christophe soon took the title of King, ruled like a tyrant, and was finally killed (1820). Meanwhile Pétion and his successor Boyer conducted a generally good government in the South. In 1820, after Christophe's death, Boyer reunited the Republic. But his government became more and more authoritarian and he had to go into exile.

Four presidents followed within three years. Of these, those who were not illiterate were very poor administrators, and the country sank deeper into confusion and chaos.

President Soulouque, elected in 1847, was no less ignorant than the worst of his predecessors. Himself a Negro, he was always suspicious of mulattoes, and repeatedly led or allowed massacres of those who were not of pure African blood. In 1849, he had himself crowned Emperor by a priest at Port-au-Prince. Finally, as was to be expected, rebellion broke out and the self-styled Emperor had to flee into exile.

After Soulouque, and until July, 1915, Haiti had seventeen presidents. Of these, only one — Nissage-Saget (1870-1874) — was able to complete his term of office and step down peacefully. Two died of natural causes while in office. All others were deposed by violence, or even killed. Often the overthrow of a government was followed by a massacre or a mass execution of those who had been — or were thought to have been — its followers.

Finally, the disorder led to an intervention by the United States. The marines landed in July, 1915, and took charge of the situation without any armed resistance whatsoever. The following month President Dartiguenave was elected, and three years later a treaty was signed that gave the United States the right to intervene in Haiti in case of further political disorders, and even placed various aspects of government under direct American supervision. In return the Constitution of 1889 was amended, and the clause was eliminated that forbade the holding of property by foreign owners — a condition in which American economic interests were clearly present. Oddly enough, the new constitution was approved through a plebiscite — a fact that shows that Haitians, in spite of their nationalism, were tired of the chaotic state of affairs.

After the American intervention, and due partly to the continued presence of American troops, three successive presidents were able to complete their terms of office. The last of these, Vincent, arranged for the peaceful withdrawal of the Americans, which was completed in 1934.

After a brief interregnum, Lescot became President of the Republic, only to return to the old despotic ways of earlier rulers. He altered the Constitution to prolong his term of office and was finally overthrown by a general strike.

From then on, the history of Haiti is a checkered course of moderately able governments and tyrannical despots. In 1968, at the time of this writing, Haiti was ruled by Duvalier, who managed the country as if it were his private farm, and who had no tolerance for opposition of any kind. Once again there seemed to be no way out of the existing situation except armed and violent revolution.

Economically, independent Haiti did not fare much better than it did politically. The previous prosperity of the French colony had been such only for the white planters, and even for them it had been possible through the constant, hard, and organized toil of thousands of slaves. With the emancipation of the slaves the old order was no longer feasible. Furthermore, many of the newly freed men, equating work with servitude, ceased producing. The departure of large numbers of whites, and the massacre of most of those who remained, deprived the country of the better trained part of its population. The constant civil wars, rebellions, and wars with the Spanish in the eastern portion of the Island further contributed to the impoverishment of the country. A surprising population explosion, coupled with the success of the Dominican Republic to curb Haiti's expansion to the East, made the country the most destitute in Latin America, and indeed one of the most underdeveloped countries in the world. At the time of this writing, the mismanagement of a long series of self-seeking governments gave no reason to hope that conditions would soon change — at least not peacefully.

The cultural and spiritual picture of independent Haiti completes the bleak picture outlined by its political upheavals and its economic woes. Again, the illiteracy rate was one of the highest in the world, and its public school system one of the worst in the New World.

Religiously, independent Haiti — as well as colonial Haiti — has been plagued by Voodooism.[2] Although Voodooism also exists in Brazil,[3] to some extent in Cuba,[4] and in vestigial form even in the South of the United States,[5] only in Haiti has it become a dominant force, not only in religious sentiment, but even in political and social matters.

Voodooism originated in Africa, in the region of Dahomey. As there was an active slave trade in that region, and as the Dahomeans proved to be the dominant group in Haiti, their religion persisted in the new environment, and even gained the allegiance of those slaves who came from other parts of Africa. This does not mean, however, that Voodooism is a unified religion with anything like a common dogma or a common priesthood. On the contrary, it varies from region to region within Haiti, and its priests usually hold authority only over their own neighborhood.

Voodoo priests — *papalois* — and priestesses — *mamanlois* — have enormous prestige among their followers, and can do as they please. This obviously results in all forms of exploitation and debauchery.

Under the leadership of its *papalois* and *mamanlois,* Voodoo worship revolves around offerings to the spirits and ritual dances. These spirits are not the Supreme God, the maker of

---

2 Besides Verschueren, *op. cit.,* Vol. III, see R. A. Loederer, *Voodoo Fire in Haiti;* M. J. Herskovits, *Life in a Haitian Village;* F. Huxley, *The Invisibles;* H. Courlander, *Religion and Politics in Haiti.*

3 P. Verger, *Notes sur le culte des Orisa et Vodun à Bahia;* D. Amorim, *Africanismo y espiritismo;* R. Bastide, *O candomblé da Bahia.*

4 F. Ortiz, *Los negros brujos.*

5 N. N. Puckett, *Folk Beliefs of the Southern Negro.*

the world, who is distant from mankind. The spirits are the forces that control nature and daily human life. Thus Dambala is the spirit of water, Legba rules fertility and all sorts of entrances, Ogoun is master of war, and Agoué controls the seas. The offerings made to these spirits vary according to the nature of the spirit one wishes to propitiate. Some are satisfied with "dry" — that is, bloodless — food, and thus receive eggs, bread, corn, beans, etc. Others require blood, and to them animals are sacrificed — a white hen to Dambala, a red rooster to Ogoun, or a black kid to Guedé. In some rare instances children have been known to be sacrificed, although human sacrifices are forbidden and have been punished by death.

The ritual dances are usually accompanied by a heady rhythm and by heavy drinking. Often one or more dancers are "taken by a saint," and speak as if they were one of the spirits, all the while moving frantically. In some cases, those possessed dance on the fire and do not appear to feel any pain. When he deems proper, the *papaloi* has the power to restrain the possessed — which shows how far his authority extends.

Magic — both white and black — is an integral part of Voodooism. There are hundreds of secret and archaic formulas by which the sorcerers claim to be able to cure all sorts of illnesses. Divining the future is widely practiced. Black magic, which attempts to harm an enemy through indirect or mysterious means, takes many forms. There are those who claim to have the power to pronounce a malediction for a fee. Others make the famous "Voodoo" dolls using objects closely related to their enemies, and believe that by harming the doll they can injure their enemy. Finally, stories of zombies and sorcerers who turn into beasts are common and widely believed — indeed, some non-Voodooist observers claim to have seen persons drugged in such a way as to seem to be "walking-dead."

Haitian Voodooism is not always wholly distinct from Catholicism. The ancient African spirits are equated with Christian saints and worshiped with Christian rituals. Thus Legba, ruler of all entrances, is Saint Peter, who holds the keys to heaven. Often in Voodoo ceremonies Catholic chants are intoned by a person specially commissioned to do so. Crosses are often found before Voodoo temples, and some sacred oaths are taken on the cross. It is common for a *papaloi* to direct his followers to light candles in church or to have masses said. Christian baptism and marriage are universally practiced, and usually accompanied with a Voodooist ceremony, or at least with festivities of Voodooist origin.

The power of Voodooism in Haiti is overwhelming, especially in the interior of the country. In many regions the word of the *papaloi* is law. Those who attempt to resist him find that their crops are mysteriously trampled, or that their animals die of some unknown cause. In the cities, where there is a higher level of education, Voodoo is not as powerful, but even there those who do not fear the curse of a sorcerer are relatively few.

There is no doubt that Voodooism, as much as anything else, has marred the image of Haiti, has prevented its cultural, economic, and political development, and has hindered the work of missionaries, Catholic as well as Protestant.

The Catholic Church in Haiti has developed within this context of political instability, economic hopelessness, and religious obscurantism. And it shows the marks of its struggle.

When Haiti became independent, the Catholic Church in that country, which had always been in very poor condition, reached the lowest point in its decline. Dessalines, the reader will remember, ordered all whites killed except priests and doctors. In spite of this several priests were killed in the South, and all but three churches were burned. The chaos that preceded and followed the declaration of independence led many priests to flee the country. Others — especially those in authority — felt that their allegiance to France made it morally mandatory that they leave.

In fact, although not in theory, Dessalines became head of the Haitian Church. He set the boundaries of parishes and appointed and transferred priests as he saw fit. This was highly irregular, and Rome resented this usurpation of authority; but there was nothing it could do as long as it was not willing to acknowledge the seemingly precarious independence of the new country.

Meanwhile Haiti continued being officially Catholic, for all its constitutions declared Catholicism to be the religion of the country, although granting tolerance to other faiths.[6]

In these circumstances the Church fell into a state of prostration, and Voodoo cults, which had always continued to exist below their Catholic varnish, once again gained the upper hand.

Finally, in 1860, a *Concordat* was signed between Haiti and the Holy See. In spite of some minor interruptions and irregularities, usually connected with violent political upheaval, this agreement — and some further clarifications of it — ruled the relations between Church and State in Haiti until the twentieth century was well advanced. The basic terms were that the Catholic Church would enjoy the protection of the State; that the President of the Republic would have the right to appoint the archbishop and bishops; that their canonical institution and consecration would be in the hands of the Church; that the State would pay them; that the bishops would rule the Church and appoint the priests; and that the establishment of new religious orders would not take place without the President's consent.

Under the protection of the *Concordat,* Haiti was organized into an ecclesiastical province with its archbishop in Port-au-Prince, and four other bishops. However, two of these sees remained vacant until 1928, when they received their first bishops.

This hierarchical organization did not suffice to create a strong Church, for in 1962, out of 278 diocesan priests, only

---

6 J. L. Mecham, *Church and State in Latin America: A History of Politico-ecclesiastical Relations,* pp. 341-344. In 1822 Haiti conquered Santo Domingo, and this gave the Haitian Church a measure of contact with the Catholic hierarchy at large, through the duly constituted archbishopric of Santo Domingo.

84 were Haitians, whereas there were 187 Frenchmen, 3 Americans, 2 Belgians, and 2 Canadians.[7] Furthermore, all those working in the local curia, in seminaries, and in national administrative functions were French, and even in the parish ministry almost 53 percent of the Haitian priests were mere coadjutors.[8] The proportion of priests in relation to the total population declined constantly from 1912 to 1944, and then began showing a slight increase. In 1959 there were 7,400 inhabitants for every priest — which points to the very limited pastoral attention that the average Haitian could expect from the Catholic Church.[9]

On the other hand, the Catholic Church — and especially the religious orders — has made a great contribution to the education of the people. In 1954 they had 403 schools, with a total enrollment of 55,380.[10]

In summary, the history of the Catholic Church in Haiti is the story of a Church long present in a country, claiming the nominal adherence of the vast majority of the population, and still unable to uproot the ancestral beliefs of its people, nor to show enough vitality to raise its own clergy and leadership. It is a Church that has survived by means of constant injections of foreign personnel.

Whereas Haitian Catholicism has its origin and main source of aid in France, Protestantism in that country has originated mostly through contact with the British and Americans. The influence of the French Reformed is felt, however, in the use of their literature and music.

Protestant work in Haiti began in 1807, when the British Methodists sent their first pastors to the country, not so much to work with the French-speaking population as to serve the

---

7 I. Alonso and G. Garrido, *La Iglesia en América Central y el Caribe*, p. 25.

8 *Ibid.*, pp. 25-26.

9 *Ibid.*, p. 40.

10 W. J. Gibbons, ed., *Basic Ecclesiastical Statistics for Latin America*, p. 43.

large numbers of English-speaking Negroes who went to the Black Republic in search of greater freedom.[11] Nine years later, while the country was still divided between the rival governments of Pétion and Christophe, the British Methodists obtained the approval of both governments to work on the Island.[12] The reason for this was that Britain had gained a great measure of prestige in Haiti through its campaign against the slave trade as well as through its advanced educational methods. In Haiti as in South America, the Lancasterian method of education was the key with which Protestantism opened many doors.

John Brown and James Catts, the first two missionaries to the South, began their work in a traditional way, combining teaching with preaching. As their teaching of the basic subjects was very much needed, there was no great objection to it. Their preaching, however, attracted large crowds, and in consequence attracted also the attention of many who believed that Protestantism was among the worst evils that could happen to Haiti. Soon a campaign was organized against the missionaries, and in 1818 they were expelled from the country on the grounds that one of those who frequented the Methodist Church had committed a crime, and that in any case the civil authorities could not take responsibility for the safety of the missionaries. Yet, this did not destroy their work, which they left in the hands of two local leaders. Thus, the British Methodist Church has continued existing in Haiti, although its growth has been moderate. In 1962 it had 2,149 members.[13] In spite of its relatively small size this Church has made a significant contribution to the education of the country. One of its missionaries, working with a local university professor, devised a system for writing Creole, and this in turn opened the way for a vast literacy campaign that taught thousands how to read. Impressed by this campaign, the govern-

---

11 P. Damboriena, *El protestantismo en la América Latina*, II, 104.

12 C. Pressoir, *Le Protestantisme Haïtien*, pp. 73-108.

13 *World Christian Handbook, 1962*, p. 117.

ment took an interest in the education of the people in Creole, and this resulted in a veritable revolution in the country's educational system.[14]

In 1816 the Quakers Etienne de Grellet and John Hancock visited the country with a missionary purpose. Their success was astounding. President Pétion gave them his full support. He even suggested that Grellet preach in the Catholic Church. Grellet had his misgivings about such a procedure, but was finally persuaded by the local priest. On that occasion, and on several others, he preached to multitudes. However, after he and Hancock returned to New York there was no one left in Haiti to continue their work.[15]

Baptist work in Haiti was begun in 1823, when the Massachusetts Baptist Missionary Society sent its first missionary to that country — Mr. Thomas Paul, of Boston. His work, however, did not prosper. The Free Baptists and the Baptist Missionary Society in London also began and later discontinued missions in Haiti. Finally, in 1923 — a century after Thomas Paul's arrival — the American Baptist Home Missions Society sent its representatives to that country, which was then under American intervention. Although this Society began its work at a relatively late date, it has been most successful, for in 1962 there were more than thirty thousand Christians who called themselves Baptists as a result of this enterprise.[16] This movement has gathered strength to such a point that it is possible to speak of a mass conversion, and is one of the most interesting phenomena of Haitian Protestantism.

Among the other Baptist groups, the largest is the Jacmel Baptist Church, which is the result of the efforts of the

---

[14] *World Christian Handbook, 1949,* p. 110.

[15] Pressoir, *op. cit.,* pp. 51-72. Grellet was really a wandering missionary with the ambition to preach the gospel in every nation. This gave him glorious moments, not only in Haiti, but also in Russia and other countries. But his work had very little continuity, or none at all.

[16] *World Christian Handbook, 1962,* p. 117.

London Baptist Missionary Society, later continued by the Jamaica Baptist Missionary Society.[17]

By far the most interesting episode in the history of Haitian Protestantism is the origin of the Episcopal Church in that country. That origin is to be found in 1861, when 110 American Negroes emigrated to the Black Republic with the hope of finding there better living conditions than were theirs in the United States. This, however, was not their only purpose in establishing themselves in a new country. They were also moved by a missionary goal: to bring Christianity as they knew it to the Republic of Haiti. Their leader was Episcopal pastor James Theodore Holly, who six years earlier had already visited the island country in order to explore the possibilities of establishing a mission there.

The first few years were full of tragedy and hardship.

> In eighteen months malaria and typhoid had carried away 43 of the immigrants — among them, five of the eight members of Holly's family. The rest of the group broke up. Some left for Jamaica, others returned to the United States, and only twenty — Holly among them — remained in the country.[18]

In 1862 Holly made a brief visit to the United States in order to awaken the interest of the Episcopal Church in the work in Haiti. As a result of his efforts, in October of 1863 the American Church accepted the responsibility of overseeing the work begun by Holly, and placed the newly born Church under the provisional jurisdiction of the bishop of Delaware. When that bishop visited Haiti the following month, he found thirty-six persons ready for confirmation. There were also several candidates to orders who were receiving instruction from Pastor Holly.[19]

---

17 Its membership is reported at three thousand in 1949, in 1957, and in 1962. Either this Church has ceased to grow, or its statistics are grossly inadequate. The latter is most probably the case.

18 J. E. Millien, "Une idée du premier cinquentenaire de l'Eglise Episcopale d'Haïti: 1861-1911" (unpublished manuscript at the library of the Episcopal Seminary of the Caribbean, Carolina, Puerto Rico), p. 7.

19 *Ibid.*, pp. 10-11.

In 1874, the General Convention of the Episcopal Church decided to grant autonomy to the new church, which was given the name of Apostolic Orthodox Haitian Church. Two years later, in New York City, Holly was consecrated as bishop of Haiti, an office he filled with distinction until his death in 1911. Meanwhile the Church had continued to grow, and it had almost two thousand members and a dozen priests.[20]

When Bishop Holly died, the Haitian clergy asked that their Church become a missionary district of the Protestant Episcopal Church. The reason for this was that they felt that they did not have the leadership necessary to be an independent body. This request was accepted by the General Convention of 1913, but meanwhile the Haitian Church had fallen into a chaotic state from which it could not begin to recover until 1923.[21] That was the year when Harry Roberts Carson was named and consecrated the first missionary bishop of Haiti. A tireless worker, Carson reorganized the Church, rebuilt the Church of the Holy Trinity in Port-au-Prince, and brought into the country the order of the Sisters of Saint Margaret, who have made a splendid contribution in the field of education. When Carson retired in 1943, he left behind a duly organized Church that was growing at a moderately rapid pace.[22] He was succeeded by Bishop Voegel, who led the Church in Haiti well into the second half of the twentieth century.

In 1964 the Episcopal Church of Haiti had almost fourteen thousand confirmed members.[23]

Besides the groups already mentioned, several others work

---

[20] *Ibid.*, pp. 11ff. Also *A Short History of the Episcopal Church in Haiti*, pp. 4-5.

[21] W. Dalzon, "Coup d'oeil sur l'histoire de l'Eglise Episcopale d'Haïti: 1911-1938" (unpublished manuscript at the library of the Episcopal Seminary of the Caribbean, Carolina, Puerto Rico), pp. 4-17.

[22] *Ibid.*, pp. 17-26. *A Short History . . .*, pp. 5-6.

[23] The *Journal de la Soixante-douxième Convocation de l'Eglise Episcopal d'Haïti* (1964) gives the total of 13,867.

in Haiti, notably the Church of God (Cleveland), the Church of the Nazarene, the Assemblies of God, the West Indies Mission, the Haiti Inland Mission, and the Unevangelized Fields Mission.[24] These, as well as dozens of minor groups, provide for the complicated picture of Protestantism that is characteristic of Latin America. As in the rest of Latin America, the bulk of Protestantism in Haiti is formed by the Pentecostals, who are, however, divided into so many groups that it is impossible to trace their history with any degree of accuracy within this brief compass. Their phenomenal growth is much more evident among the lower urban classes than elsewhere, and is of a relatively recent date, having begun in the 1940s.

Of all the countries in the Latin Caribbean, Haiti has the greatest number of Protestants. The Protestant community was said to include 327,140 members in 1961, which would mean that Haiti had the fifth largest number of Protestants in Latin America — after Brazil, Mexico, Chile, and Argentina — and 4.23 percent of all Protestants in the whole continent.[25] In recent years the growth of the Protestant community has more than kept pace with the growth of the population, for in 1952 only 3.23 percent of all Haitians were Protestants, and nine years later 9.12 percent had embraced the Protestant faith. Apart from Chile (11.80 percent), this is the highest percentage of Protestants in all Latin America.[26]

Pastors are very scarce in Haiti, for there are 2,138 believers for every minister.[27] But at the same time one must point out that 87 percent of these pastors are nationals — a proportion surpassed only by El Salvador, Brazil,[28] and, after the Revolution, Cuba. Very few of them have had a solid theological education, for there are no Protestant seminaries

24 Damboriena, *op. cit.,* pp. 108-110.
25 *Ibid.,* p. 29, cuadro 20.
26 *Ibid.,* p. 25, cuadro 14.
27 *Ibid.,* p. 27, cuadro 18.
28 *Ibid.,* p. 23, cuadro 12.

in Haiti, and most ministerial candidates either have no formal training at all or take a brief course in a Bible institute. After 1961 the Episcopal Church has been sending its candidates to the Episcopal Seminary of the Caribbean in Puerto Rico.

There are many lessons that can be drawn from the history of Christianity in Haiti; but these are better left to be discussed in the concluding chapter of this book, where it will be possible to draw also on material from the rest of the Latin Caribbean.

# VII

# THE DOMINICAN REPUBLIC

When we left the Spanish portion of Hispaniola in 1795, it had been placed under the French flag by virtue of the Treaty of Basel. Although this did not make the country independent, it was the end of the Spanish colonial regime — which was only reinstated for a brief period thereafter — and therefore seemed to be a better breaking point than the actual date of independence.

The cession of their land to a foreign power without any sort of respect for their destiny and feelings made the Dominicans acutely aware that from the point of view of Spain they were considered to be citizens of a second order. This, however, was not sufficient to give birth to a powerful sentiment in favor of independence, and for years the Dominicans looked back with nostalgia at the days when they were a Spanish colony. If the French yoke was heavy, even heavier was the Haitian one, imposed on the Dominicans in 1801 by Toussaint Louverture, who conquered the region as part of his campaign against France. The following year the

French recaptured Santo Domingo, as part of General Ferrand's campaign against the Haitians.

From 1802 to 1809 the French controlled the former Spanish colony, but at the latter date the Dominican Juan Sánchez Ramírez defeated Ferrand and once more proclaimed Spanish sovereignty over the eastern portion of the Island.

Spain, however, was too entangled in other affairs to pay a great deal of attention to this colony so graciously returned to her, and the Dominicans now began to fret under the humiliating Spanish attitude. As a result, rebellion broke out once more — although now against Spain — and the Dominicans, led by José Núñez de Cáceres, proclaimed the independence of their country and placed it under the protection of Bolivar's Great Colombia (1821).

The Haitians then, led by President Boyer, resolved to take advantage of the new situation, and once more invaded the region, took Santo Domingo, and ruled there until 1844.

In 1844 the Dominicans revolted against the Haitians and, under the leadership of Juan Pablo Duarte, Ramón Mella, and Francisco del Rosario Sánchez, once more gained their independence, which they now retained until 1861. From 1844 to 1861 two men continually fought for the presidency — Santana and Báez — with the result that the country, taken first in one direction and then in the other, made very little progress. The new Republic's financial instability created grave international conflicts, and finally, in 1861, Santana once more placed the country under the Spanish flag.

For four more years Spain proved herself unable to rule over her former colony, so that in 1865, after two years of armed revolt, the Dominicans gained their independence for the third time.

Apparently, however, the Dominicans were not able to manage their own affairs much better than the Spaniards, for political strife rose to such a level that very few governments were able to complete their terms of office — there were twenty presidents between 1863 and 1916 — and those that did, such as Ulises Heureaux, overextended their stay and became tyrants.

Early in the twentieth century, after a prolonged civil war, the United States intervened militarily in the Dominican Republic as it had done in Haiti. The Americans ruled from 1916 to 1924, and even then they retained certain control over Dominican economic affairs. This intervention, however, did not succeed in bringing peace to the country, for its eventual result was the rise to power of Rafael Leónidas Trujillo, one of the worst tyrants that the New World has seen, who ruled the country for over three decades.

Trujillo's assassination did not bring peace to the country, but another period of instability and civil strife — now mostly between the armed forces and the political left — which in turn resulted in another American military intervention (1965). After that intervention President Joaquín Balaguer was elected. But there were no indications that the hatred that had developed through years of tyranny and foreign military intervention would not explode once more into a new and more violent revolution.

The Catholic Church suffered the consequences of the political troubles of the country. The archbishopric of Santo Domingo has frequently been vacant for long periods: 1797-1817; 1830-1848; 1866-1885; 1932-1935. Usually these periods corresponded to times of political unrest, when Rome did not know what kind of man would be needed to cope with the situation, or when political conditions or foreign control made it impossible duly to elect an archbishop. Thus, for instance, during the time of Haitian government, as Haiti was in the midst of a conflict with Rome over the question of the "patronato," the Dominicans found themselves involved in a virtual schism for which they were not responsible.[1] In at least one occasion, when Archbishop Nouel became President, members of the hierarchy have helped solve political

---

[1] This is one of the reasons why the motto of those who fought for independence was "Dios, patria y libertad" — God, country, and freedom.

conflicts. At other times, and especially during Trujillo's reign, they have been accused of being too lenient and co-operative with tyrannical governments.

From the beginning of independence in 1844, and well into the twentieth century, all the various constitutions of the Dominican Republic have granted to Roman Catholicism the category of religion of the State, but they have also guaranteed freedom of worship. In contrast with most other countries of Latin America, the question of the national "patronato" — that is, the question of the succession of national governments to the ecclesiastical rights granted to the kings of Spain and Portugal — has never been a grave issue. In 1884 an agreement was made with the Holy See whereby the Pope appoints the archbishop out of a list of three nominees submitted by the Dominican Congress.[2]

In 1959 the territorial organization of the Church was revised, resulting in one archdiocese — Santo Domingo — three dioceses — La Vega, Santiago de los Caballeros, and Nuestra Señora de Altagracia — and a *nullius* prelature — San Juan de la Maguana.[3] Obviously, "missionary" work is concentrated in the prelature, although this does not mean that the inhabitants there are not Catholic, but only that the Church is not yet organized in a permanent fashion. All the priests working in parishes in San Juan de la Maguana are foreigners. So are all the regular priests working in parishes in the whole country. Of the diocesan priests, approximately two-thirds are Dominicans. Most of the foreign diocesan priests are Spaniards, whereas Canadian priests are more numerous among the regulars.

Apparently the population increases faster than the number of Catholics, although the difference is not great — between 1935 and 1950 the population increased by 44.37 percent, while the number of Catholics went up 43.85 percent.[4]

2 Mecham, *Church and State in Latin America,* pp. 349-354.
3 Alonso and Garrido, *La Iglesia en América Central y el Caribe,* p. 71.
4 *Ibid,* p. 85.

The weakest point that statistics show in the development of the Catholic Church in the Dominican Republic is the recruitment of a native priesthood. While it is true that in recent years the number of priests in the Dominican Republic has increased faster than in any other country of Latin America, this increase is due to the presence of more foreign priests, and not to new and more numerous sacerdotal vocations among the Dominican youth.[5] As in all the countries of the Latin Caribbean, the Catholic Church has proved unable up to the present to capture the imagination of its youth in such a way that local leadership can be brought up. This is tragic, not only in its direct consequence in lack of priests, but also in what it shows as to the degree of vitality of that Church.

Protestantism entered the territory of what is today the Dominican Republic during the period of Haitian occupation. In 1824 the President of Haiti, Jean Pierre Boyer, decided that it would be wise to stimulate the immigration of American Negroes who would help populate the Island and improve the methods of agriculture. The first group of immigrants settled in Samaná and Puerto Plata in 1824. Later they grew in numbers and scattered throughout the whole of the Samaná Peninsula. As these American Negroes had taken their faith with them, and now felt that they needed religious leadership, they requested that pastors be sent from the United States and England. Thus, in 1834 the first Methodist pastor arrived from Britain. Slightly later he was followed by an American colleague belonging to the African Methodist Episcopal Church. From then on, Methodist services have been held in the region, congregations have been organized, and churches have been built. Early in the twentieth century services began to be held in Spanish, although the English services were not discontinued for a long time.[6] In 1957 the African Methodist Episcopal Church had 1,800 members, and the Free Methodists had 1,406.[7] However, the vast majority

---

5 *Ibid.*, p. 86.

6 E. A. Odell, *It Came to Pass*, pp. 146-147.

7 Damboriena, *El protestantismo en la América Latina*, cuadro 39.

of those who would otherwise have been Methodist had joined the Evangelical Dominican Church, to whose origin we now turn.

Missionary work to Santo Domingo on the part of Protestants began due to the initiative of Puerto Rican Protestants and of the missionaries who worked with them. In 1911 the Presbyterian Church in the city of Mayagüez, on the western extreme of Puerto Rico — and therefore very close to the Dominican Republic — offered to contribute to missionary work in the neighboring country. Slightly later the Evangelical Union of Puerto Rico — a forerunner of the actual Evangelical Council of Puerto Rico — sent two representatives to the Dominican Republic in order to investigate what possibilities there were for missionary work there. This visit was followed by that of three Puerto Rican Bible colporteurs. In 1916 the Executive Committee of the Evangelical Union decided to request the help of the various missionary boards in the United States for the evangelization of the Dominican Republic. They also appointed a local committee that was to organize a board to direct missions to Santo Domingo with the cooperation of Congregationalists, Disciples, Methodist Episcopalians, Presbyterians, and United Brethren. The final result of all this was the organization in 1920, in New York, of the Board for Christian Work in Santo Domingo, with the participation of the Methodist Episcopalians, Presbyterians, and United Brethren.[8] At that time this Board was a unique missionary experiment without precedent in the history of missions. Never before had various denominational boards of missions come together with the purpose of establishing in a foreign country a single Church, united from its very beginning.

During its first years the new work in the Dominican Republic was under the direction of Dr. Nathan Huffman, who had previously served as a missionary in Puerto Rico and had been one of the leading spirits in the conception of this new

8 *Ibid.,* pp. 148-149.

united effort. His first three pastors were all from Puerto Rico, sent as missionaries by the churches in the neighboring island — Alberto Martínez, José Espada Marrero, and Rafael Rodríguez. They concentrated their work in the capital, San Pedro de Macorís, and La Romana. From then on, these three cities have been focal points in the development of the Dominican Evangelical Church.

The Board for Christian work in Santo Domingo was interested, not only in strictly evangelistic work, but also in medical services, rural reconstruction, and education. In 1932 the International Hospital was founded in the city of Santo Domingo. For a quarter of a century this institution served as one of the most prestigious centers for the training of nurses in the country. When the government developed medical services in the capital to such an extent that the Board felt that its institution there should be closed, new medical centers were opened in Barahona and in two of the slums of Santo Domingo. The old hospital became a school that made a significant contribution to the education of the country. Another very interesting and rather singular aspect of the educational work of the Evangelical Dominican Church is its bookstore, the Librería Dominicana. Not only has this establishment been for many years the most important bookstore in the country, but it has been much more than a bookstore. As a publishing house it has printed and distributed, not only Christian books, but also a large number of Dominican authors that would otherwise have remained unpublished. Furthermore, during the frequent and prolonged periods of oppression and intellectual stagnation, the literary and cultural soirées of Librería Dominicana were the one place where the most distinguished intellectuals of the country could meet and exchange ideas.[9]

The Iglesia Evangélica Dominicana became autonomous in 1955. Since then the local representatives of the Board for

---

9 W. L. Wipfler, "The Churches in the Dominican Republic in the Light of History" (unpublished thesis presented to the Faculty of Union Theological Seminary, New York, 1964), pp. 165-174.

Christian Work in Santo Domingo would no longer be superintendents of all the life of the Church, but would serve rather as contacts between the national Church and the Board in New York. Previously, successive steps had been taken to prepare the Church for autonomy — especially the training of ministers and laymen who would be able to carry greater responsibilities.[10]

In 1963 the Iglesia Evangélica Dominicana had 27 organized churches, 19 ordained pastors, 155 other workers, and a total membership of 3,300.[11] If one takes into consideration the fact that a few years earlier the Moravians had decided to join the Dominican Church, and that they brought into that Church two congregations with 120 members,[12] and also the fact that many of the former Methodists of various branches joined the united Church, one is surprised by the slow rate of growth of a Church that had so auspicious a beginning. This is probably due, in part at least, to the continuous effort to build an organization with all the characteristics, personnel, and facilities that are found in the mother churches in the United States. In consequence a great deal of energy is spent in institutional matters, and organization becomes a hindrance rather than a help.

The Episcopal Church was planted in the Dominican Republic in the nineteenth century, when a number of persons belonging to that denomination were attracted to the island country by its policies intended to draw immigrants. In 1898 they sent a request to Bishop Holly, of Haiti, asking him to ordain their first pastor — the Reverend Benjamin I. Wilson. Although his congregation was entirely composed of English-speaking persons, Wilson showed great interest in winning their Spanish-speaking neighbors. Therefore he held

10 Most of these pastors were trained either at the Evangelical Seminary of Puerto Rico or at the Union Theological Seminary of Matanzas, Cuba. Both of these are interdenominational institutions that will be mentioned again when dealing with Cuba and Puerto Rico.

11 Wipfler, *op. cit.*, pp. 177-178.

12 Damboriena, *op. cit.*, cuadro 39.

services in Spanish from the very beginning of his ministerial career.[13] The Episcopal Church in the United States, however, paid very little attention to the Dominican Republic, at least until the time of the American occupation. Even then the American Episcopal Church centered its attention on the military and other Americans who were now on the Island, and neglected, not only the Spanish-speaking work, but also that among the English-speaking Negro immigrants from the West Indies, in spite of the fact that many of these were Anglican in their background. For a long time there was hardly any episcopal supervision, for the Dominican Republic was placed first under the bishop of Puerto Rico, and later under the bishop of Haiti, and neither of these had the necessary time to devote to the neighboring country. Therefore each missionary established his own policies, and these often contradicted each other. Under such circumstances the Episcopal Church grew very slowly during the first half of the twentieth century.[14]

Spanish work was begun anew in 1952, through the initiative of the Reverend Mr. Thomas O. Basden, a native of the British West Indies who was the only local pastor ordained in thirty-five years.[15] Although English was his mother tongue, Basden began preaching in Spanish in Puerto Plata, and since then the Episcopal Church in the Dominican Republic has continued to grow, while it has also lost a great deal of its markedly foreign character. However, in spite of its many forward steps, this Church has not yet been able to regain the time that was lost, especially in the recruiting of native leadership. In 1957 it had nine places of worship, a thousand members, and only one Dominican pastor.[16] After that time a bishop has been appointed, and a great deal of attention is being given to the recruitment of candidates for the ministry, who are sent to acquire their theological edu-

13 Wipfler, *op. cit.*, pp. 130-131.
14 *Ibid.*, pp. 132-146.
15 *Ibid.*, p. 147.
16 Damboriena, *op. cit.*, cuadro 39.

cation at the Episcopal Seminary of the Caribbean in Puerto Rico.

Apart from the denominations that have already been mentioned, there are very few that can boast of any sizable membership. Actually, in 1957 only three claimed more than a thousand members: the Church of God of Cleveland (1,-099), the Christian Missions in Many Lands (1,400), and the Seventh-day Adventists (3,198).[17]

From all the foregoing it is quite obvious that Protestantism has made relatively small numerical inroads in the Dominican Republic, although it has made significant social and cultural contributions. In 1961 Dominican Protestants were only 1.61 percent of the total population of the country,[18] and only 68 percent of all Protestant pastors there were native Dominicans.[19] In both cases these are the lowest percentages in the Latin Caribbean. In all there were 19,289 Protestants in the Dominican Republic in 1961.[20]

---

[17] *Ibid.*, cuadro 39.
[18] *Ibid.*, cuadro 14.
[19] *Ibid.*, cuadro 12.
[20] *Ibid.*, cuadro 5.

# VIII

# CUBA

DURING THE LATTER PART OF THE NINETEENTH CENTURY CUBAN national sentiment had been growing, and repeated conspiracies, rebellions, and even wars had taken place. The last of these wars, begun in 1895, was still raging in 1898 when, after the mysterious sinking of the battleship Maine in the harbor of Havana, the United States declared war on Spain. In that war the Cubans considered the American forces their ally, and lent them their full support. In the siege of Santiago, which was the decisive battle, the Cubans, under General Calixto García, took charge of besieging the city from the west, of thwarting several attempts by the Spaniards to send in reinforcements, and of clearing the beaches for the American landing east of the city. When, slightly later, Spain surrendered to the United States, the Cubans rejoiced in what they considered also their victory.

This mood was not long lived, however, for in 1901, while the Cuban patriots were writing the Constitution of the nation, the American Congress voted the "Platt Amendment," which required that before independence was granted to the Island, the American government was to be given the right to intervene in the new nation in case of political disturbances, the right to establish naval bases on the Island, and the assurance that no other foreign power should be granted land for such bases. This infelicitous declaration of Congress had to be appended to the Cuban Constitution of 1901, against the will of the Constitutional Assembly, as the price for cessation of American occupation.

The twentieth of May of 1902 Cuba was declared independent, and its first President, don Tomás Estrada Palma, took the oath of office. Estrada Palma was a man of great integrity who led the nascent republic with wisdom and honesty. His reelection, however, was not met with universal approval, and in 1906 a rebellion broke out. Not being a man of arms, and not wishing to shed the blood of his compatriots, the President took a most unpopular step: he requested American intervention. Then, not wishing to be an obstacle in the reconciliation of his country, he resigned, together with the Vice President and the entire Cabinet. This in fact left the country headless, for Congress refused to meet in order to appoint a new head of government. Under such circumstances the American government appointed Mr. Charles E. Magoon to govern the Island until order could be restored and a new President elected. Mr. Magoon's administration had evil consequences for Cuba, for it was he who did away with the scrupulous financial policies of Estrada Palma and began using public funds for political purposes. When he received his authority, Cuba had fourteen million dollars in reserve, whereas at the end of his office there were eight million dollars of debts. From this time on, bad administration and the use of public funds for private or party political ends have been among the worst evils in Cuba.

In 1909 the Second American Intervention ended, and José Miguel Gómez became the second President of the Republic. From then on, Cuba had three duly elected presidents, until the last of these, Gerardo Machado, decided to have the Constitution revised so as to extend his period of office. This caused a revolution which overthrew Machado in 1933, but which was unable to create a stable government, and thus opened the way for a period of constant political changes that ended in 1940, when Fulgencio Batista became President — although he had been a power in Cuban politics since the coup of September 4, 1933. From then on, and until the time of Batista's second coup — March 10, 1952 — Cuba had two other duly elected presidents. These governments, however, did little to restore the people's confidence in democracy, for their corrupt administration was almost unbelievable.

In 1952 Batista once more made use of the army to gain power. Although the people had very little respect for the government that he overthrew, his action was inexcusable, for elections were only a few months away and he now threw the country into a state of political confusion that was to have most unfortunate consequences. Furthermore, Batista's rule soon became one, not only of illegality, but also of abuse and oppression. As opposition grew, there being no legal channels for it, it took the form of conspiracy, to which Batista's henchmen responded with imprisonment, torture, and murder.

These were the circumstances that gave rise to Fidel Castro's popularity. Through a series of well-planned maneuvers he became identified with the opposition to Batista. Although he was not by any means the only leader of that opposition and his was not the only organization working against the government, he had such renown that by January, 1959, when Batista fled the country, he was able to seize power without any opposition whatsoever.

Once in power, Castro's first move was to dissolve all revolutionary groups but his own. Then he embarked on a nationalistic campaign which easily grasped the imagination of most Cubans, high and low, and which gave him occasion to destroy in the name of nationalism many who were beginning to oppose his purely personal government. After a few months the nationalistic revolution took a turn toward a social revolution — first the enemy had been the "batistianos," then they were the Yankees, and now the enemy was all rich and higher middle-class Cubans. Finally, the revolution that had begun with the assertion that it was "as Cuban as the palm trees" came to form part of world Communism and became fixed and petrified by the dogmatic requirements of Marxism-Leninism. Meanwhile the national economy had been totally disrupted, Cuba had lost its world credit, thousands of Cubans had died, and hundreds of thousands had gone into exile.[1]

In varying degrees the history of the Catholic Church in Cuba has reflected the changing political situation.

In 1898, when Spanish rule over Cuba came to an end, there was widespread anticlerical feeling in the Island. The main reason for this was the almost unanimous opposition of the clergy to Cuban independence, and their staunch support even of the most extreme repressive measures taken by the Spanish government. This anticlerical feeling, however, did not manifest itself in actions of violence against the Church, mostly because most Cubans still felt that they were loyal Catholics, because the years of American interregnum

---

[1] No mention has been made in this last paragraph of the United States because there are different interpretations as to the extent to which their policies precipitated events in Cuba. Some claim that the economic crisis in Cuba is the direct result of the American embargo. Others go even further and declare that American policy pushed Castro into Communism. I believe that both of these interpretations exaggerate the importance of the United States in recent Cuban events. Long before the embargo was declared, Castro had already brought upon himself an almost total international embargo by refusing to pay foreign accounts, thereby losing all international credit. It was after the embargo, when Russia came to his aid, that Castro was able to regain some of that credit. As to the other possibility that American policy may have pushed Cuba toward Communism, there is no doubt that repeated attitudes and decisions on the part of the American government pushed Cuba in that direction. But I believe that by the time of Batista's last months all those mistakes had been made, and that there was nothing the United States could have done to make Castro change his course of action.

served as a buffer to hold back the radicals, and because many of the Spanish priests, who would have been singled out for violence, left the country.

Due in part to the loss of prestige of the Church during the last years of the nineteenth century, and in part to their own convictions, the Cuban patriots never claimed for the new government the inheritance of the rights of *patronato* that the Spanish crown had had over the Church. Thus, a great cause of conflict — and one that for years plagued many Latin-American nations — was avoided. For the same reasons the Constitution of 1901 declared that Church and State were to be absolutely separated and that there was to be freedom of worship.[2]

The state of clear decline into which the Church had fallen during the last years of Spanish rule continued after Cuba became independent. The shortage of priests, their meager education, and the lack of understanding of the Catholic faith on the part of the laity were the main problems that confronted that Church during the first two decades of the twentieth century.

It was during the next decade that the Catholic Church began showing signs of new life. This was mostly the result of the work of Catholic Action. At that time the number of Cuban priests began to rise slowly, new orders and lay movements were introduced from abroad, and a large number of schools and other institutions of social service were founded.[3] Notable among these was the Universidad de Santo Tomás de Villanueva, which soon gained great prestige in various academic fields.

The result of this growth was that in 1954 there were in Cuba 719 priests (208 diocesan and 511 religious) and 1,939 women in religious orders. There were 285 monastic houses (110 for men and 175 for women), 250 schools wth a total enrollment of 55,857, and 57 charitable institutions (orphan-

2 Mecham, *Church and State in Latin America,* pp. 354-359.

3 J. J. Considine, *The Church in the New Latin America,* p. 184.

ages, dispensaries, etc) .[4] There were one cardinal, two arch-bishops, and five bishops, all of whom were Cubans. The future of Roman Catholicism on the Island seemed assured.

There were, however, certain practices that — although quite common in other Latin-American countries — were to be the weak point at which Castro would eventually attack the Catholic Church. Such practices were the attempt to overcome the shortage of priests by importing them from Spain, thereby making the Church almost as conservative as that of the mother country, the excessive participation of the clergy in the pomp and show of unpopular governments such as Batista's, and the use of the lottery and the income of cemeteries to fill some of its financial needs.[5]

The revolution of 1959 brought in an entirely new set of circumstances. At first it seemed that the relations between Church and State would continue being what they had been since independence. There were even some conservative Catholics who hoped that the new government would give the Church greater power. But conflicts soon emerged. At first it was the matter of religious education in public schools — which the conservatives had been advocating for decades. Then there were the issues of the church properties, and especially the cemetery of Colón in Havana, which the government confiscated. Finally, it became clear that the conflict was ideological in character.

---

[4] Gibbons, ed., *Basic Ecclesiastical Statistics for Latin America,* pp. 44-45.

[5] This is clearly shown in L. Dewart, *Christianity and Revolution.* This work, however, does not present a true picture of developments in Cuba during Castro's time. In its effort to show that the hierarchy was unable to cope with the new situation — which it was — Dewart goes so far as to imply that, had the hierarchy's attitudes been different, Castro would not have turned Communist. This fails to take into consideration the lack of real prestige that the hierarchy always had in independent Cuba. Once Castro had taken hold of power, the Church was only a very minor factor in determining his policy one way or another. Actually, one could even make a case claiming that Castro's opposition has heightened the prestige of the Church, at least for some Cubans.

The exodus of Roman Catholic priests began about a year after Castro's rise to power. The first to leave in voluntary exile were two priests who had distinguished themselves in the struggle against Batista, and who therefore knew the inner maneuvers of the government. They were followed by others in ever increasing numbers, until finally the government itself began expelling priests and hierarchs by the hundreds. Among those expelled were many Cuban nationals who were sent to Spain against their will. By the end of 1961 — only three years after the beginning of the revolution — almost six hundred priests had either been expelled or forced to leave.[6] Besides, a number of Cuban laymen have been led by their Catholic convictions to oppose the government, and their lives have ended abruptly before a firing squad. Among these, Catholic leaders usually mention Carlos Matos and Arnaldo Socorro, although there have been many more.[7] Finally, all Catholic schools — as well as the University of Santo Tomás — have been confiscated, and countless churches have been desecrated.

Apart from this, it is very difficult to judge the state of Roman Catholic Christianity in Cuba, for the lack of statistics makes it impossible to have concrete data. Reports would seem to suggest that there has been a remarkable increase in church attendance. This is not surprising if one takes into consideration that before the revolution very few people thought enough of religion to attend church regularly. The revolution, by polarizing the sentiments of the people, has forced many who previously were not too deeply committed to religion to make a decision for or against it. Although this has resulted in increased opposition to the Church, it has also increased the numbers of those who have made a more definite commitment to it. Also, many whose way of life has been radically changed by the revolution, or who

---

6 *L'Osservatore Romano,* Jan. 24, 1962.

7 L. A. Aparicio, *Donde está el cadáver se reúnen los buitres,* p. 13. This book, although conservative in its outlook, is valuable for the wealth of information it offers on the persecution of Catholics in Cuba.

have lost their loved ones through death, prison, or exile, find in church life a needed support. Finally, one suspects that there are many who attend church simply because they know that the government frowns upon it, and that church attendance is thus a means of silent protest.

Although the history of Protestantism in Cuba began a long time before independence, we have chosen to discuss it here because the first permanent Protestant communities were closely connected with the events that led to independence, and in any case the greatest part of the development of Protestantism in Cuba has taken place after that time.

The first Protestant services ever held in Cuba took place in 1741, when the British occupied the valley of Guantánamo for a brief period. Similarly, in 1762, when the British took Havana, they appropriated the convent of Saint Francis and celebrated in it the Anglican liturgy. In both cases, however, Protestantism was not brought in with a missionary purpose, but simply as the religion of the invaders, and it left with them.

During the second half of the nineteenth century, seeing the growing numbers of Americans and British who had settled on the Island, the Protestant Episcopal Church of the United States began considering the possibility of sending a pastor who would minister to them. Finally, in 1871, the Reverend Edward Kenney arrived at Havana. He was the first Protestant pastor to attempt permanent work in Cuba, where he labored for nine years. Although his ministry was primarily directed to English-speaking people, he also managed to gather a small group of Cubans. When yellow fever compelled him to return to the United States, another pastor was named to take his place, but he remained in the country for only two years.[8]

The actual origins of Cuban Protestantism are to be found in the hundreds of persons who went into exile to the United

---

[8] L. J. Alard, "Proceso histórico de la Iglesia Episcopal de Cuba" (unpublished manuscript in the library of the Episcopal Seminary of the Caribbean, Carolina, Puerto Rico, 1966), pp. 11-16.

States during the period of almost continuing struggle for independence that began in 1868. In Key West, Tampa, Philadelphia, and New York there were large Cuban communities among which Protestants soon began to work. There soon were some young Cuban exiles who decided to become ministers, received their theological education in the United States, and became pastors of Cuban churches in exile.

It was in these exile churches that the interest soon developed to evangelize Cuba. As at that time Spain was under a liberal government that permitted such visits, in 1882 the Cuban Protestants in the United States began sending some from among their number to Cuba, there to distribute the Scriptures and to explore the possibilities of opening missionary work.

The most remarkable of these envoys was the Episcopalian Pedro Duarte, who did not content himself with distributing the Scriptures, but went further, and in 1884 gathered in the city of Matanzas a congregation to which he gave the name of "Fieles a Jesús" — Faithful to Jesus. Duarte's success led other Protestant Cubans in the United States to increased interest in the evangelization of their homeland. One such person was the Reverend Juan B. Báez, pastor of the Cuban Episcopal congregation of Key West, who visited Matanzas repeatedly, and finally was able to arouse the interest of the bishop of Florida. Meanwhile Duarte himself, after spending some time in the United States to pursue theological studies and be ordained, extended his work to several cities in the western half of Cuba. Quite naturally his work aroused the opposition of the local authorities, both civil and ecclesiastical, and Duarte himself had to spend some time in prison because of his faith. Finally, as tension between Cubans and Spaniards grew worse, and as war threatened to break out, Duarte was forced to leave the country. This, as well as the ensuing war, scattered most of his congregations. Only a small group in Havana continued meeting regularly throughout the war.[9]

9 *Ibid.*, pp. 17-31.

The American intervention in the war with Spain changed this state of affairs. Cuba was provisionally placed under an American government, and this awakened the Episcopal Church to its missionary opportunities there. Duarte and several other Episcopalians who had gone into exile were able to return. The scattered congregations were gathered once more, and in 1900 there were already in Cuba two Episcopal missionaries and three native pastors. Schools and orphanages were founded in Havana and Matanzas. In 1901 the General Convention of the Protestant Episcopal Church declared the Missionary District of Cuba to be officially constituted.[10] In 1902, when a bishop was named for Puerto Rico, he was also given jurisdiction over Cuba. In 1904, two years after independence, the first bishop of the Missionary District was elected — the Very Reverend A. W. Knight.[11]

After the appointment of its first bishop the Episcopal Church in Cuba continued to grow and develop, at least until the revolution of 1959. In 1951 it joined the efforts of the Presbyterians and the Methodists in the Union Theological Seminary in Matanzas. The number of native pastors was steadily growing, and more responsibility was progressively being placed on their shoulders until the first native bishop was consecrated — the Very Reverend Romualdo González.

The revolution of 1959 seems to have affected this denomination more than others, for in 1957 it had 8,634 communicants,[12] and in 1965 their number had been reduced to 3,712.[13] Besides, all its schools and other charitable institutions had been confiscated by the government.

Presbyterian work in Cuba is almost as old as that of the Episcopalians, and is also the result of the work of Cubans

---

[10] This is significant because until that time there had been no official acknowledgment of work in Cuba, for there were those in the Episcopal Church who did not consider this predominantly Catholic country a proper field for missions.

[11] Alard, *op. cit.*, pp. 34-42.

[12] Damboriena, *El protestantismo en la América Latina*, cuadro 27.

[13] *Diario de la quincuagésima séptima Convocación Anual de la Iglesia Episcopal en la Diócesis Misionera de Cuba.*

who had come to know the Protestant faith while in exile in the United States. The first and most remarkable of these was Evaristo Collazo, who in 1890 wrote to the Southern Presbyterians in the United States informing them of the existence in Cuba of three congregations and a school for girls that he and his wife had founded and supported until that time. In answer to Collazo's letter, a missionary who was currently working in Mexico was sent in a brief visit to Cuba, where he organized Collazo's congregations as Presbyterian churches. This visit was followed by that of other missionaries, and funds were sent to Collazo so that he could devote all his time to pastoral and evangelistic work. All of this, however, was interrupted by the War of Independence, when Collazo joined the Cuban armies.

After the war the Southern Presbyterian missionaries returned to Cuba, and later were joined by their northern brethren. The latter worked mostly in Havana, with the valuable help of Collazo and Pedro Rioseco — another Cuban. The most remarkable contribution of the Southern Presbyterians during this period was in the field of education, for their missionaries Margaret E. Craig and Robert L. Wharton founded in Cárdenas a school that later became very well known under the name of "La Progresiva."

In 1909 the Congregationalists, who had recently begun work in Cuba, decided to leave the Island, and their five centers of preaching were passed on to the Northern Presbyterians. In 1918 the Disciples did likewise with the three congregations and one pastor they had in Cuba — the pastor was the Reverend Julio Fuentes, later to become the first Cuban superintendent of the Presbyterian mission. As that same year the Southern Presbyterians also passed on their work to those of the North, the latter soon had a sizable Church in Cuba.[14]

During the first decades of the twentieth century Cuban Presbyterians received their theological education in Mexico. Later they began to send their students to the Evangelical Seminary of Puerto Rico. Finally, in 1947, the Union Theo-

14 E. A. Odell, *It Came to Pass,* pp. 79-97.

logical Seminary was founded in Matanzas. This was at first a joint venture of the Presbyterians and Methodists, but the Episcopalians soon joined in it. In a few years, mainly through the efforts and direction of its first rector, Dr. Alfonso Rodríguez Hidalgo, it became one of the best centers of theological education in Latin America.

It is difficult to judge the effect of the revolution on the Cuban Presbyterian Church. Certainly, no other denomination has had as much division in its midst between extreme opponents and extreme advocates of Castro's regime. Finally it became impossible for those pastors who were too critical of the regime to remain in the Presbytery — and the government thereby scored its greatest victory in its effort to control the churches. This is especially surprising if one takes into account that before the revolution the Presbyterian Church had concentrated its efforts on the urban middle classes, and that many of those who then boasted most of their white-collar congregations are now those who are most outspoken in favor of the revolution.

In any case the size of the Presbyterian Church was never great, especially in view of its early origins and of the addition of Congregationalist and Disciples congregations. In 1957 they claimed 3,241 members and a "total community" — which means people touched by the Church in a more peripheral way — of 20,000.[15] In 1961 all Presbyterian schools — as indeed all private schools — were confiscated by the government. In 1967 the Presbyterian Church of Cuba became autonomous.

Methodism also entered the Island through Cuban exiles in the United States. In 1873 Pastor Charles Fulwood, of the Methodist Episcopal Church of the South, began working among the Cuban residents of Key West.[16] In 1883 the Florida Conference sent two Cuban missionaries to their own home-

---

15 Damboriena, *op. cit.*, cuadro 27.

16 S. A. Neblett, *Methodism in Cuba: The First Thirteen Years*, p. 11. In this whole section we follow closely this work by one of the most distinguished Methodist missionaries to Cuba.

land: Enrique B. Someillán and Aurelio Silvera. After gathering a small congregation that held its services in a hotel in Havana, Someillán returned to the United States and left Silvera in charge of the work in Cuba. In 1888 Silvera organized his congregation into a church that had 194 members. That same year J. J. Ransom, the first Methodist American missionary, arrived in Cuba. He was followed by several Cuban pastors from Florida: Clemente Moya, Miguel Pérez Arnaldo, and Isidoro E. Barredo.

The War of Independence which broke out between Spain and the Cuban rebels in 1895 — and which eventually developed into the Spanish-American War — interrupted Methodist work on the Island, for the Spanish government took measures against the rebels that also hindered the free movement of the Methodist preachers. At that time several Methodist leaders left the cities and joined the Cuban armies.

In 1898, after the Spanish-American War, steps were taken to begin anew the work that had been interrupted in Cuba. The war itself, as well as all the reports related to the Cubans' struggle for freedom, made Cuba an important concern in the minds of many Americans. Soldiers, doctors, and chaplains returned from the war advocating missions to Cuba. As a result, in 1898, after having sent two representatives to determine the real possibilities existing in the Island, the Florida Conference organized a missionary district that included seven centers of evangelism. Shortly thereafter several schools were founded, as well as a number of medical dispensaries in rural districts. Some of these schools were among the best in the country — such as Candler and Buenavista in Havana, Pinson in Camagüey, Eliza Bowman in Cienfuegos, and Irene Toland in Matanzas. Many smaller ones provided a good basic education in small towns where the public school system was very poor. In Matanzas the Methodist Church also participated in the Union Theological Seminary. The most remarkable of all Methodist institutions, however, was the Agricultural School at Playa Manteca, Mayarí, on the eastern section of the Island. In this institution young boys received training in modern agricultural methods, as well as in some trades that could be useful in the country, while girls learned home economics and their application to daily living in rural Cuba. Through a warm, sincere, and open Christian spirit, the school had a higher percentage of converts among its students than any other Protestant school in Cuba. A large number of its graduates, upon returning home, undertook the task of evangelizing their neighbors as well as teaching them some of the new agricultural methods. Soon there were a large number of small churches in Oriente Province, and many of their pastors were graduates of the Agricultural School. In 1961 this school, as well as all the others — except the Seminary — was confiscated by Castro's government.

Rural work was certainly the strongest aspect of Cuban Methodism. Apart from the work of the Agricultural School and its graduates in the region of Mayarí, there were several other centers around which a large number of rural churches were founded. Most notable among these were Báguanos in Oriente Province and Cienfuegos in the province of Las Villas.

In 1957 Methodism in Cuba had 8,145 members, 47 Cuban pastors, 9 men missionaries, and 39 women missionaries — of whom many were working in the schools.[17] The effect of the revolution on this Church cannot be exactly gauged, although a few general remarks can be made. As has already been said, all its schools were confiscated by the government. Of its pastors, a large number felt that they should leave the Island. Those who remained, however, were able to continue the work, and a new generation of pastors was soon forthcoming. Although there were tensions and suspicions between those who chose one course and those who chose another, these feelings did not reach the level they attained in other denominations, and communications between the two groups did not break down completely.[18] In 1968, after having obtained

[17] Damboriena, *op. cit.*, cuadro 27.

[18] Part of the credit for this goes to the late Reverend Angel Fuster, who chose — and somehow managed — to continue working in Cuba with-

the approval of the General Conference, Cuban Methodism became autonomous.

Finally, a word must be said about the growth of Methodism among exiled Cubans. Of all Protestants, the Methodists have done the most work with the exiles. As many of them feel a very real sense of loss, they are open to a new and vital presentation of Christianity. Although statistics are wanting — and it would probably be almost impossible to collect them — the number of Methodist Cubans in exile is probably approaching that of Methodists in Cuba itself.

Baptist work in Cuba is divided among the Eastern Baptists — affiliated with the American Baptists — and the Western Baptists — related to their brethren of the South. As in the case of the three denominations already discussed, Baptist work in Cuba began through the efforts of exiles who had been converted abroad. In 1883 Alberto J. Díaz, an exile who had become a Protestant in New York, returned to Cuba as a Bible colporteur. Two years later Díaz organized a small nucleus of believers which took the name of "Cuban Reformed Church," and which later established contact with Baptists in the United States. In 1957 the Eastern Baptists had 6,395 members, and those of the West had 8,315.[19] Both groups had several schools, and each had its own seminary — one in Havana and one in Santiago. In 1961 all their schools, except the seminaries, were closed down. Around that time most American Baptist missionaries left. The missionary leaders of the Southern Baptists, however, remained, and for years were very outspoken in favor of the revolution. Then suddenly Castro declared that they were the heads of the Central Intelligence Agency in Cuba, put them in prison, and demanded from the Southern Baptists an enormous amount for their ransom.

---

out thereby becoming a supporter of the government. His example has helped other Cuban pastors who are attempting to follow the same difficult path. Killed in a tragic accident in Florida, Fuster was posthumously elected by the newly autonomous Methodist Church as its first bishop.

19 Damboriena, *op. cit.,* cuadro 27.

Besides the Episcopalians, Presbyterians, Methodists, and Baptists, there are in Cuba several smaller denominations. Such are the Missouri Lutherans, the Free Will Baptists, the Quakers, the Salvation Army, the Church of God (both Cleveland and Anderson), the Church of the Prophecy, the Berean Mission, the Nazarenes, the West Indies Mission, the Assemblies of God, and the Seventh-day Adventists. There are also a number of small autochthonous fundamentalist and Pentecostal groups. Most of these denominations have suffered more under the revolution than the more historic churches. The reasons for this are mainly three: first, most of them depended to a large degree on foreign missionaries; second, they usually have a clearer and more fixed set of rules of conduct, which brings them into conflict with government policies at several points; third, they were more directly hit by Castro's general attack on religion of the thirteenth of March, 1963, when he declared that several fundamentalist sects were really agents of the Central Intelligence Agency.

In 1961 Cuba was the sixth country in Latin America in the size of its Protestant community: 264,927 members.[20] This Protestant community comprised 3.89 percent of the population — and in this respect Cuba was seventh in Latin America.[21] If one takes into consideration the relatively late beginning of Protestantism on the Island, this is a remarkable index of growth — the highest in the Latin Caribbean since 1949.[22]

What the final result of the present circumstances will be, we dare not guess. One can only trust that the Lord of History will once more turn the crooked human ways into a straight path to his ends.

---

[20] *Ibid.,* cuadro 20. The data, however, are much earlier than 1961.

[21] *Ibid.,* cuadro 14.

[22] *Ibid.,* cuadro 13.

# IX

# PUERTO RICO

As a result of the Spanish-American War, Puerto Rico, which had been invaded by American troops, remained under the American flag. At first the military government did much to improve living conditions on the Island. Roads were built, schools founded, public services organized, and sanitation greatly furthered.

During the First World War Puerto Ricans were granted American citizenship. Slowly, however, the authorities in Washington lost interest in their small possession, and conditions in Puerto Rico declined steadily. The result was that independentist sentiment, which had not been general even under Spanish rule, now began to grow.

In the late 1930s a new political power appeared on the scene — the Popular Democratic Party, led by Luis Muñoz Marín. In 1940 that party won the elections — for the legislature, as the governor was appointed by Washington. It immediately launched a program of social and political reform that culminated in the Constitution of 1952. This document, approved by the American Congress and by the people of Puerto Rico, turned the Island into a Commonwealth — the Spanish title was *Estado Libre Asociado* — closely related to the United States, but with a great degree of autonomy. At present Puerto Rico elects its own government, makes its own laws, and determines its own taxes, but is united to the federal government in its foreign policy, its submission to the federal Constitution and all federal laws, the postal, financial, and Selective Service systems, and federal customs — although the Island also collects its own taxes from certain imports from the United States. The economic level of the Island, while higher than any other Latin-American nation, is lower than that of any state in the Union. This situation is somewhat alleviated by the various federal welfare programs that apply in Puerto Rico.

The state of the Catholic Church in Puerto Rico immediately after the Spanish-American War was very poor. Before the war the general decay had been stalled to a degree by the constant arrival of priests who had left the new Latin-American republics because they felt that their loyalty to Spain compelled them to do so. With the end of Spanish rule the number of priests began declining. In 1930, when the Church — and Puerto Rico in general — was at its lowest level, there were only forty-five diocesan priests. At that time, and until 1950, there was a slow increase. Finally, in 1955, the number of diocesan priests reached the same level at which it had been in 1910. This great lack of secular priests was remedied by bringing in great numbers of religious priests, almost all foreign.[1] In 1962 there were four hundred priests, of whom 86 were diocesan and 314 were religious.[2] Of the 400 priests, only 48 were natives, and the rest were mostly Americans (151), Spanish (148), and Dutch (33).[3] In the early 1960s none of the bishops was Puerto Rican, but this situation changed radically toward the end of the decade, when all the

---

[1] Alonso and Garrido, *La Iglesia en América Central y el Caribe,* p. 59.

[2] *Ibid.,* p. 47.

[3] *Ibid.,* p. 51.

positions of higher responsibilities were occupied by natives of the Island.

Apart from its parish work the Catholic Church in Puerto Rico has a large number of schools — mostly manned by members of religious orders, several minor seminaries, a major seminary in philosophy in Ponce, and one in theology in Bayamón — under the Dominican Fathers. There is also the Catholic University in Ponce, which has grown at an enormous speed and has an extension in Bayamón, near San Juan.

The first Protestant services to be held in Puerto Rico took place in 1598, when the British took San Juan and held it for five months. One can also conjecture that in 1625, when the Dutch landed on the Island and bombarded San Juan for four days, Protestant services were held among the attackers. But these were only very brief incidents in a long history in which the Holy Office, the restriction of commerce, and the ban on all foreign immigration kept Puerto Rico from having direct contact with Protestantism. Thus, when in 1846 the Board of Commerce and Development requested from Spain that non-Catholic foreigners be allowed to settle in Puerto Rico, the government agencies in Madrid, following the recommendation of the bishop of San Juan, refused to grant the authorization requested.[4] This, however, did not keep a few Protestants from settling on the Island, for in 1866 General Marchesi thought that a special section in the cemeteries should be assigned for the burial of Protestants.[5] It is also recorded that in 1853 a Danish sea captain introduced in Humacao a "Children's Primer" in which the influence of Protestantism was detected.[6]

Apart from these isolated incidents, the origins of Protestantism in Puerto Rico are to be found in the second half of the nineteenth century, after the Spanish Revolution decreed religious tolerance in 1868. The two earliest centers of Prot-

---

4 L. Cruz Monclova, *Historia de Puerto Rico: Siglo XIX*, I, 422-431.
5 *Ibid.*, p. 571.
6 *Ibid.*, p. 644.

estantism were Ponce — a city in the South of the Island — and Vieques — a small island off the eastern shore of Puerto Rico.

In 1869 the first service was held in Ponce by a Reformed minister from the neighboring island of St. Thomas. More than two hundred persons attended. Four years later, as the Reformed Church had not followed up on its work, the Anglican Church organized a congregation in Ponce, and built in that city the first Protestant church building in Puerto Rico. The first pastor in Ponce, the Reverend Alfredo Giolma, was followed by the Reverend Zacarías Vall Espinosa, a very able preacher and controversialist under whose leadership the Ponce congregation grew to four hundred members.[7]

The work in Vieques was begun by the Dutchman Johannes Waldemar Zechune, who opened a school there and gathered congregations in Vieques as well as in Fajardo, Luquillo, and Naguabo. In Vieques also an Anglican Church was organized, although it did not develop as rapidly as the one in Ponce.

After the Spanish-American War it seemed advisable to transfer the nascent church in Puerto Rico to the jurisdiction of the Episcopal Church in the United States. This latter church then sent two missionaries to Puerto Rico, one to work in San Juan and the other in Ponce, where the existing church was practically abandoned after Father Vall Espinosa's retirement.[8]

In 1902 the Reverend James Heartt Van Buren, rector of the parish of San Juan, was elected as Puerto Rico's first missionary bishop. From then on the Episcopal Church continued to grow and to develop deeper roots in the land, so that in 1964, with the election of the Very Reverend Francisco Reus Froylán, the Episcopal Church had its first Puerto Rican

---

[7] *Ibid.*, pp. 852-853.

[8] V. Burset, "The First Fifty Years of the Protestant Episcopal Church in Puerto Rico" (unpublished manuscript in the library of the Episcopal Seminary of the Caribbean, Carolina, Puerto Rico), p. 29.

bishop.[9] At that time the Episcopal Church had over three thousand members.[10]

An interesting episode in the development of the Episcopal Church in Puerto Rico was the addition to that body of the "Iglesia de Jesús" — Church of Jesus — founded in 1902 by Manuel Ferrando. Ferrando was Spanish in origin, but had come to Puerto Rico as a chaplain in the American army. After the war he settled in Quebrada Limón, near Ponce, and there he gathered a congregation and trained pastors and deaconesses to serve in the church he was building. He also founded an orphanage. When, twenty years later, the Church of Jesus joined the Episcopal Church, it had a bishop (Ferrando himself), four priests, and more than two thousand members.[11]

In 1961 the Episcopal Seminary of the Caribbean was founded in Carolina, a few miles east of San Juan. It serves, not only Puerto Rico, but the entire Caribbean — including Central America, Panama, and Colombia.

Although the Presbyterians arrived in Puerto Rico in 1899, they profited from events that had begun to take place as early as 1868. At that time Antonio Badillo Hernández visited Saint Thomas and there obtained a copy of the Bible. After returning to Puerto Rico, he studied his new acquisition, and felt led by it to Protestantism. He then began leading his friends and relatives in the same direction. When he died, his teachings did not succumb, but rather were continued by his widow and children. In consequence, in 1900, when the Presbyterian missionary Judson L. Underwood visited the town

9 M. Arce Trías, "Consagran primer obispo nativo de la Iglesia Episcopal de Puerto Rico," *El Debate,* IV, Núm. 189 (1964), p. 3.

10 That is, it had 3,236 in 1957 (Damboriena, *El protestanismo en la América Latina,* cuadro 38).

11 These data are taken from an unpublished and anonymous manuscript to be found in the library of the Episcopal Seminary of the Caribbean. My attention was drawn to it by Dr. Donald Moore, who has made a thorough study of Protestant origins in Puerto Rico, and to whom I owe many of the data for this chapter.

of Aguadilla, he found there a group who called themselves "believers in the Word" whose doctrines were clearly Protestant. This was the first nucleus of the Presbyterian Church in Puerto Rico.[12]

Apart from Badillo Hernández and his group Presbyterian work in Puerto Rico was begun in 1899, when the first missionaries arrived. Previously, the Presbyterian Board of Missions had made agreements with other boards to work in different regions so that the various denominations would not overlap and compete with each other.[13] This is the reason why Presbyterian work in Puerto Rico is centered around the city of Mayagüez, on the western end of the Island. They have also worked in San Juan, where they founded the Presbyterian Hospital — for years the most prestigious medical institution in Puerto Rico.

Early in their missionary efforts the Presbyterians founded in Mayagüez a center for training pastors. In 1919 they joined several other denominations for creating the Evangelical Seminary of Puerto Rico, whose first president was the Presbyterian missionary Dr. James A. McAllister.

In 1964 there were in Puerto Rico fifty-two Presbyterian Churches, and they had slightly over six thousand members.[14]

The Lutheran pioneer in Puerto Rico was a young seminarian, Mr. G. S. Swensson, whose daring work compelled his denomination to send missionaries to Puerto Rico.

When this young man learned of the change of sovereign-

---

12 B. Badillo Bello, "Influencia de una Biblia," *Puerto Rico Evangélico*, 10 de oct. de 1915, p. 17; M. A. Valentine, "Antonio Badillo Hernández," *La Voz Presbiteriana*, mayo de 1960, p. 11.

13 This comity agreement included also the Philippines and Cuba, although it was not carried out in Cuba. Originally the denominations involved were the Presbyterians, American Baptists, Congregationals, and Methodist Episcopalians. Later other denominations joined in it. D. T. Moore, "Puerto Rico para Cristo," pp. 23-26; R. P. Beaver, *Ecumenical Beginning in Protestant World Mission*, pp. 134-136; A. J. Brown, *One Hundred Years*, pp. 862-863.

14 *Minutes of the General Assembly of the United Presbyterian Church in the United States of America, 1965.*

ties which had taken place in Puerto Rico, he felt an ardent desire to come to this island to preach the Gospel. Like those crusaders of the faith of ancient times, young Swensson left his studies and, with no more moral or material support than his own Christian fervor, and only five dollars in his pockets and a Bible in his hands, he boarded the American merchant ship "Arcadia" and left for Puerto Rico. On October 5, 1898, the valiant pioneer of faith arrived at San Juan.

Towards the end of October of 1899 the first two Lutheran missionaries arrived in Puerto Rico. They took official charge of the work which had already begun, and young Swensson remained as their assistant until September of 1902, when he returned to the United States in order to continue his studies for the ministry.[15]

In spite of having begun its work at such an early date, Lutheranism did not grow very rapidly in Puerto Rico. For years there was a great shortage of candidates for the ministry among young Lutheran Puerto Ricans. By the late 1960s there were signs that this situation was improving. In any case the statistics of 1957 show 2,265 Lutherans in Puerto Rico.[16] Apart from their usual church work the Lutherans have made a great contribution to Protestantism in general through their bookstore, "La Reforma," which is the main distributor of Protestant books in Puerto Rico.

The American Baptists sent their first representative to Puerto Rico early in 1899. Their first missionary was Hugh P. McCormick, who established his center of activities in Río Piedras, a few miles south of San Juan. There he held the first service the twenty-eighth of February of 1899, and the success of his work was such that the Baptist Church in Río Piedras became one of the largest on the Island.[17] This was due, not only to Mr. McCormick, but also to the succession of very able leaders that that church had — among them the

---

15 J. L. Delgado, in an unpublished manuscript kept by the First Baptist Church of Río Piedras, Puerto Rico, "Introducción," pp. 13-14.

16 Damboriena, *op. cit.,* cuadro 38.

17 Delgado, *op. cit.,* cap. 1, pp. 10-12.

Reverend Francisco Colón Brunet, who was its pastor for more than forty years. Another remarkable missionary was A. Bartholomew Rudd, generally known in Puerto Rico as "don Bartolo." He extended Baptist work to a number of towns and rural areas in the neighborhood of Río Piedras.

The Baptists, like most other denominations, founded several educational and charitable institutions in Puerto Rico. Of these the most important was probably the Baptist Academy in Barranquitas. In 1928 the Baptists of Puerto Rico sent out their first missionary, who went to El Salvador.[18] However, this zeal for missions to other lands has not continued through the years. In 1957 there were 6,176 Baptists in Puerto Rico.[19] In 1968 their leadership and other circumstances were such that one would feel inclined to say that this was one of the denominations with a clearer future in Puerto Rico.

The United Evangelical Church was the result of the union of the United Brethren, the Christian Church, and the Congregationalists, which took place in 1931.[20]

The United Brethren began their work in Puerto Rico in 1899, when Nathan H. Huffman took residence in Ponce. A year later the first congregation was organized. In 1901 Mr. Huffman received Philo W. Drury as his fellow worker. Drury was a man of great vision who was concerned for the evangelization of all the South of Puerto Rico as well as for the united witness that all denominations should present. After his arrival, churches were founded in many towns around Ponce. In a few years Puerto Rican converts were leaving as missionaries to the Dominican Republic. Meanwhile Huffman and Drury had advocated closer collaboration with other

---

18 C. S. Detweiler, *The Waiting Isles: Baptist Mission to the Caribbean,* p. 53.

19 Damboriena, *op. cit.,* cuadro 38.

20 The section on the Evangelical United Church has as its sources J. Díaz Acosta, *Historia de la Iglesia Evangélica Unida de Puerto Rico,* and A. Arturet, "Desarrollo histórico de la Iglesia Evangélica Unida de Puerto Rico" (unpublished manuscript in the library of the Evangelical Seminary of Puerto Rico, Río Piedras, Puerto Rico).

denominations, and were even discussing the possibility of some organic union.

The Christian Church arrived in Puerto Rico in 1901, and it also began its work in Ponce. Its diffusion was not as great as that of the Brethren, nor was its growth as rapid. Near Ponce it founded churches in Santa Isabel and Salinas. In 1912 it erected its first church building in Ponce.

The Congregational Christian Church also arrived in Puerto Rico early in the twentieth century. Its main operations were in the eastern end of the Island, where it built strong congregations in Humacao, Yabucoa, and Fajardo. It also worked in Santurce, just south of San Juan, where it founded in 1907 the Blanche Kellogg Institute — for many years one of the most prestigious educational institutions in Puerto Rico.[21]

In 1931 these three denominations came together in the "Iglesia Evangélica Unida de Puerto Rico" — United Evangelical Church of Puerto Rico. At that time they declared:

> Moved by the firm and deep conviction that the will of Christ is that those who believe in Him be efficaciously united in love and in their efforts for the extension of His Kingdom, and that a real and true union of denominational forces will result in greater glory for our Lord and will bring greater benefits in the salvation of souls and in the establishment of a Christian social order on our Island, the three denominations, Congregational, Christian and United Brethren in Christ, in Puerto Rico, solemnly unite and thus form the United Evangelical Church of Puerto Rico.[22]

This union was the result of the effort of several leaders both in Puerto Rico and abroad — among them, as was to be expected, Philo Drury. It was hoped that this union would result in more rapid growth in all aspects of church life. This, however, was not so. Quite the contrary, the United Evangelical Church moved more slowly than any of its three compo-

---

[21] During the Second World War the Institute closed down and its properties were sold to the government.

[22] Quoted by Arturet, *op. cit.*, pp. 143-144.

nents had done. In the number of their membership, for instance, in 1930 the three separate denominations had 3,518 members;[23] in 1957 the United Church had 4,931.[24] The slowness of this growth is probably due to the inner difficulties that arose in the Evangelical United Church because many of the issues posed by the union were not solved beforehand, but were left to be solved as the various situations arose. Thus, there developed conflicts among those who were previously members of different denominations. This negative experience is probably the reason why the United Evangelical Church, which had as one of its original goals to continue working toward organic union with other bodies, soon abandoned that goal and became simply one more denomination alongside others.

Methodism came to Puerto Rico in 1900, with the missionary Charles W. Drees. His work was based in San Juan, and from there it eventually extended westward to Arecibo. Later, work was also begun in the Southeast in and around the town of Guayama.[25] Education was always an important concern of Methodist leaders. This resulted in the founding of a large number of schools in various towns. As public instruction improved, however, many of these schools closed down, and Methodist educational interest was concentrated in a few urban centers — notably in Robinson School in Santurce. Besides founding schools the early Methodist pastors showed their concern for the people's education through vast literacy campaigns and other programs of adult education. After the first few years, however, a change took place in the character of Methodism that is difficult to explain. It became more entrenched and more clerical, while at the same time receiving a great amount of financial help from outside. Thus, in spite of having the best physical facilities of any Protestant denomination in Puerto Rico, its growth has been scant. In 1957 admittedly inflated statistics showed that the Methodist

---

23 *Ibid.,* p. 131.

24 Damboriena, *op. cit.,* cuadro 38.

25 *El Defensor Cristiano,* April 1, 1910, pp. 14-16.

Church, in spite of having 71 workers of various kinds, had only 4,675 members.[26] In 1968, after almost seventy years of existence, Puerto Rican Methodism was finally organized into a full Annual Conference.

The first Disciple missionaries to Puerto Rico were Mr. and Mrs. J. A. Erwin, who came to the Island in 1899. Two years later Erwin became a District Judge for Puerto Rico, and he and his wife were succeeded in their missionary tasks by Mr. and Mrs. W. M. Taylor. In seven years there were two organized churches and five other preaching points or missions.[27] From then on, the Disciples have continued to grow. In 1933 they opened conversations for organic union with the Evangelical United Church, but the union never took place. A few years later there was a wave of Pentecostal influence that swept some congregations, and its mark could still be seen decades later in the worship of some congregations and the nature of the piety of some Disciples. In 1957 there were 6,283 Disciples in Puerto Rico.[28] They and the Baptists were the two most dynamic non-Pentecostal denominations on the Island.

The Assemblies of God — known in Puerto Rico as the Iglesia de Dios Pentecostal — are by far the largest and fastest-growing denomination on the Island. In 1957 they had 9,895 baptized members,[29] and, contrary to the historical churches, their growth was still accelerating. Their origins are not to be found in the work of missionaries from the United States, but in a group of Puerto Ricans who went to Hawaii in search of better living conditions early in the twentieth century. Almost all of them were Catholic, but many became related to Protestant churches in Hawaii. It was there that Juan L. Lugo and Salomón Feliciano had their first Pentecostal experiences — although Feliciano had already been bap-

---

26 Damboriena, *op. cit.*, cuadro 38.

27 G. K. Lewis, *The American Christian Missionary Society and the Disciples of Christ*, p. 140.

28 Damboriena, *op. cit.*, cuadro 38.

29 *Ibid.*

tized in the Methodist Church of Ponce, Puerto Rico. In 1916, while living in San Francisco, Lugo had a vision in which he felt transported to a high hill from which he could see the city of Ponce. Taking this vision as a call from the Lord, Lugo decided to go and preach the gospel in his native land.[30] There he worked jointly with Salomón Feliciano, who had had in Hawaii and in San Francisco experiences similar to those of Lugo — although he felt ultimately called to the Dominican Republic. The work of Lugo and Feliciano grew rapidly, mostly because there were a great number of converts from Catholicism, but also because several groups that had broken off from other churches joined it. This was the case in Ponce, where there was a split within the Methodist Church, and a number of its former members joined the Pentecostals. In Arecibo there already was a splinter group which called itself the "Puerto Rican Church," and which also joined the Assemblies of God.

This, however, does not mean that the very rapid growth of the Assemblies of God — as well as of other Pentecostal groups — is due to proselytism from other Protestant denominations. Quite the contrary, there seem to be more Pentecostals who join the historic churches than vice versa. The extremely rapid growth of Pentecostal groups is due rather to the stress that is laid on the constant witness of every believer. This witness consists in talking of the gospel at all times and places, but it also includes very clearly defined rules of conduct — which some people find reassuring in the midst of all the confusion of the modern world.

It is interesting to note that while the historic churches are talking and experimenting on a "tent-making ministry," the Iglesia de Dios Pentecostal — as the Assemblies of God are called in Puerto Rico — has had this type of ministry for years. Also, one should note that this denomination in Puerto Rico is completely self-supporting, and that it has missionaries in at least nine Latin-American countries, as well as Spain and Portugal.

---

30 J. L. Lugo, *Pentecostés en Puerto Rico.*

It was out of the Iglesia de Dios Pentecostal in Arecibo that the Mita movement was born. Mita is a goddess who claims to be the incarnation of the Holy Ghost, and who has been able to gather thousands of followers.

Besides the denominations that have already been mentioned, there are countless smaller groups working in Puerto Rico. The Defenders of the Faith have several churches and a seminary on the Island, and they have extended from it to the Dominican Republic. The Mennonites have a few churches, and in the town of Aibonito they have a hospital and a Bible institute. Other groups are the Church of God (Cleveland), the Church of the Nazarene, the Christian Missionary Alliance, the Salvation Army, the Pilgrim Holiness Church, and the Seventh-day Adventists.[31]

Most of the historic denominations have shown interest in the coordination of their work. In 1905 this interest resulted in the formation of the Federación de Iglesias Evangélicas de Puerto Rico, which included Baptists, Congregationals, the Christian Church, Disciples, Methodists, Presbyterians, and United Brethren. This federation was instrumental in the founding of *Puerto Rico Evangélico,* a Protestant periodical of an interdenominational character. In 1916, implementing the resolutions of the Panama Congress, the Federación became the Unión Evangélica de Puerto Rico. As the Federación helped establish *Puerto Rico Evangélico,* the Unión made a valuable contribution in coordinating ideas that resulted in the Evangelical Seminary of Puerto Rico, founded in 1919. The Unión Evangélica was followed in 1934 by the Asociación de Iglesias Evangélicas de Puerto Rico, and in 1954 by the Concilio Evangélico. Although interdenominational work has always continued in Puerto Rico, around 1935 there was a general decline of interest in organic union, which previously had been an important objective of many Protestant leaders. By the late 1960s such union was rarely

---

[31] Statistics regarding their membership can be found in Damboriena, *op. cit.,* cuadro 38.

discussed, and, even then, only within the context of the various union negotiations taking place in the United States. As for the Concilio Evangélico, it was going through crises the outcome of which it was impossible to foretell.[32]

In concluding this brief survey of the development of Protestantism in Puerto Rico, there are two remarks that may be of value:

First, it is necessary to note that in Puerto Rico, and to a greater degree than in any other country in Latin America, Protestantism was able to reach all economic, social, and political spheres. There are Protestants among rural people and urban laborers as well as in the highest levels of political and academic life. In 1961, 7.4 percent of the population was Protestant.[33]

Second, one should note that the historic churches in Puerto Rico, which fifty years ago were leading the whole Protestant world in entirely new ventures, such as the creation of a united Church in the Dominican Republic, and which were able to develop a union such as that which resulted in the United Evangelical Church, have lost a great deal of their renewing and missionary impetus. To some extent that impetus was taken by the Pentecostal movement, so that Puerto Rico soon became a center radiating Pentecostal missions to several countries.

---

[32] There is an outline of the history of the Evangelical Council in M. Sáenz, *Economic Aspects of Church Development in Puerto Rico,* Appendix D, pp. 171-172.

[33] Damboriena, *op. cit.,* cuadro 14.

# PART THREE

# CONCLUSION

# X

# THE LESSONS OF THE PAST AND THE CHALLENGE OF THE FUTURE

BEFORE WE ATTEMPT TO EVALUATE THE STORY THAT HAS BEEN told in the preceding chapters we must point out what are our criteria for such evaluation. These criteria are mainly two — growth and relevance. Although some church leaders tend to emphasize one or the other to such an extent that its counterpart loses importance, it is our conviction that both of these are fundamental aspects of the mission of the Church, and indeed that real growth implies relevance and vice versa.

Relevance is essential to the mission of the Church due to the nature of the gospel it proclaims: the gospel of the God who made himself relevant, not only in the history of Israel and the nations, but also and foremost in Jesus Christ. As God does not simply tell us what to do without becoming one of us, so can the Church not tell the world what to do and wherein it will find its salvation without sharing in the anguish and hopes of the world. The object of Christian proclamation is not to pull people out of the society in which they

115

have been placed by God, but rather to reconcile them with God and their neighbor so that the will of God may be done in that society. Thus, the measuring of church development merely in terms of numerical growth does not give a total picture of a Church's obedience to its mission.

On the other hand, relevance without growth is nonsense, both practically and theologically. Theologically, because the New Testament clearly shows that God's plans include the formation of a body of believers who give witness to him, but who also gather together to "break the bread," and to whom God adds "those who are to be saved." Any interpretation of the mission of the Church that has no room for this aspect of it implies a twisted understanding of the gospel itself. Practically, the claim to relevance without growth is nonsense because it is difficult to see how a body can be relevant to its situation and still not attract others who wish to join it, or at least hear its message. Granted that there may be extreme situations — Nazi Germany, for instance — in which relevance that is obedient to the gospel requires alienation from the vast majority of society, it is still true that churches in such situations are relevant if they speak, not with the self-righteousness of those who consider themselves correct, but with the same spirit of witness that in more normal circumstances leads to church growth.

Thus we may reasonably assume that these two criteria give us a fair view of the work of various denominations in the Latin Caribbean, and that taken as joint objectives they may lead the way into the future. This is clearly an oversimplification for the sake of clarity, but one that is not altogether wrong, especially if we add a third criterion whose presence is difficult to measure, but whose absence is readily manifest: reconciliation. This is even more important as there are churches in the Latin Caribbean that are divided between those who argue for relevance and those who argue for growth — divided in such a way that there is no witness to reconciliation, and therefore neither growth nor relevance!

For the purposes of this evaluation we can discuss Christianity in the Latin Caribbean under four headings: Catholicism, Fundamentalism, Pentecostalism, and the historic Protestant churches.

The criterion of church growth is difficult to apply to Catholicism in the Latin Caribbean, for it has always claimed almost the totality of the population. Relevance is also difficult to gauge, for there are many different attitudes among Catholic leaders. It would be fair to say, however, that Catholic relevance in the Latin Caribbean reached its lowest ebb at the time of the end of the old colonial regimes. At that time the Catholic Church was undeniably linked with powers and social structures that were neither popular nor justifiable by the gospel. Much later — in some cases in the early 1940s, and in some others not until the 1960s — the Church took great steps of renewal. Such were the founding of Catholic Action groups, Catholic Worker Youth, the Daughters of Mary, and several other lay movements. These groups often opposed social and political injustices, especially in Cuba, where many of their members became leaders of the opposition to Batista and later to Castro. The hierarchy, however, seldom spoke out on controversial issues of a social or political nature (in Cuba, however, they spoke out valiantly against Castro's excesses, and the leader of this policy was expelled) ; in Puerto Rico they adopted a reactionary attitude toward the Partido Popular Democrático and were crushed at the ballots, with the result that their highest ranking men were transferred. The Second Vatican Council came to strengthen the forces for renewal, and in the late 1960s it was clear that they were gaining the upper hand in Puerto Rico and, to some extent, in Cuba. The situation in Haiti and the Dominican Republic was not as advanced.

The issues confronting Roman Catholicism in the Latin Caribbean in the second half of the twentieth century vary from country to country. In Cuba they are the issues of obedience to the gospel within a totalitarian regime. In Puerto Rico they are the issues of how a Catholicism that has been closely tied to a culture can survive the emergence of new cultural and social patterns, and how it can influence those patterns for the good. In Haiti the issue is how the Church can show its concern for the freedom of the people — freedom from political oppression as well as from poverty and ignorance — and how it can lead its followers to a Christianity purified from superstition and idolatry. In the Dominican Republic the issue is what the Church is to do within a socially and politically instable country. Is it to promote revolution, with the hope of better conditions, and the danger of chaos and greater injustice? Or is it to promote stability, with the hope of social and political improvement, but the danger of stagnation? All of these issues are more crucial for the Catholic Church than for Protestants, for it at least has large numbers of followers whose attitudes can make a great difference in their countries.

Although Fundamentalism as a theological position is quite common among Pentecostals and among members of the historic Protestant churches, under this heading we are including a great number of denominations which are neither historic nor Pentecostal, and which often like to describe themselves as Fundamentalists. These groups, although many, are usually small. They tend to grow mostly among the lower classes. They usually have fixed answers for most problems, and herein lies their attractiveness for some people. Their code of conduct is usually very detailed and highly moralistic, often with a great preoccupation about sex. They find it difficult to collaborate with the historic denominations, which they like to call "liberal," and often some minor point of doctrine separates them also from other Fundamentalist groups. Their size and theology make it difficult for them to say or do much about the world around them, but condemn it. These are the groups with the smallest following and the least relevance in the constantly changing scene of the Latin Caribbean. As for reconciliation, they often consider strict orthodoxy in some minor point to be above it, and therefore they often witness to self-righteous correctness rather than forgiving reconciliation.

It is in the Pentecostals that Protestant numerical strength lies in the Latin Caribbean. Almost nonexistent thirty years ago, they are by far the majority of Protestants, and their rate of growth still seems to be accelerating. This growth is due to many factors. They work mostly among the lower classes, who are less inhibited in talking about their own experiences and feelings, and who therefore become constant missionaries to their neighbors and friends. To strengthen this characteristic, Pentecostal worship and preaching constantly dwell on the responsibility on the part of every Christian to witness for Christ. While the historic churches have been discussing cultural indigenization, the Pentecostals have taken guitars and maracas and made them instruments of worship. While the historic churches have been talking about greater participation by the laity in worship, the Pentecostals have made worship an act of the whole congregation — granted, with what seem excesses to middle-class taste, and what some might call emotional self-stimulation, but also usually with a great degree of sincerity. While the historic churches have been talking about self-support, and creating structures that make that goal more and more distant, the Pentecostals have let their institutional life develop "as the Spirit sees fit." This makes for a great deal of confusion, and more often than not Pentecostals end up with structures that are very similar to those of the historic churches; but they are structures that have evolved out of the need for them, and not out of some preconceived ideas as to what constitutes a mature church.

It is often said that Pentecostals, in spite of all this, have very little relevance for the actual life of the Latin Caribbean and, indeed, for the whole of Latin America. It is true that Pentecostals usually tend to teach an ethics of separation from the world, that they do not have a social creed, and that they discourage their members from participating in politics. On the other hand, it is difficult to see how a movement that is totally irrelevant to the human situation can have the surprising growth that is so characteristic of Pentecostalism. Therefore, it would be true to say that Pentecostalism in the Latin

Caribbean, while being very relevant to the individual concerns of a large number of persons, has not shown any great interest in the social, political, and economic issues that must be decided in the very countries in which it is developing so rapidly. This situation, however, is bound to change, even if only because the Pentecostal movement will soon have enough members in some countries of the Latin Caribbean to become a political factor. At that time its traditional aloofness from political issues will most probably break down. Then Pentecostals will be forced to discuss and decide what their faith implies for their political action. Meanwhile it would be well to point out to those of us who belong to the more "socially concerned" churches, that no other denomination has as much contact with, or is doing as much for the lower classes of the Latin Caribbean, as the Pentecostals.

Thus, the future of Protestantism in the Latin Caribbean may well lie with the Pentecostals, although there are also some obstacles in their way that we would do well to point out. The first of these is their divisive character. Pentecostal churches tend to divide repeatedly. Some larger Pentecostal denominations have overcome this. Those that do not will be left aside as Pentecostals are led toward greater influence in the shaping of society. Another obstacle is the cultural barrier. Only as more Pentecostals become educated will they be able to provide leadership for the future. Can a better educated person share with the same fervor in a Pentecostal service? There are many who cannot, and leave their church for one of the historical denominations. Others seem quite able to continue within the Pentecostal tradition, although they usually tend to advocate more moderate and orderly worship. There is no doubt that, as they rise in the social scale, Pentecostals will try to worship in a more sedate manner. Will this destroy their zeal and their growth? Many within the Pentecostal movement believe it will, and are therefore suspicious of education. Thus, the only way that seems to be open for the movement is to try to find means by which those who become educated can still find in it their spiritual home. If

Pentecostalism continues to show the flexibility that has characterized it, this should not be impossible.

The growth of the historic Protestant churches was rapid during the first decades of the century, but has since slowed down to the point that several of them are hardly growing at all, and many are not keeping up with the population explosion. During the early decades of the century, when they were having their greatest growth, these churches also had a relevance in society that was greater than their numbers would lead one to expect. This was effected through schools, hospitals, bookstores, rural centers, and other such institutions that promote the welfare of the people. By mid-century, however, the various governments in the Latin Caribbean — prompted in part by the example of Protestant institutions — were taking over the responsibility for the education, health, and general welfare of the people. It is true that government schools and hospitals were poor and insufficient, but even so they were more numerous — and in some cases better — than religious institutions, with the result that the latter began losing their claim to a service that no one else would render. Many schools and hospitals were closed or sold. Others were going through financial difficulties due to reduced missionary budgets in the United States. No substitute for these institutions was found, and thus the churches had no effective way to show their concern for the people.

At the same time growth in membership slowed down. Although the reasons for this are subject to conjecture, one could argue for the thesis that this was the direct result of the missionary policies followed by these churches. Indeed, it was supposed that the object of missions was to plant churches and to lead them to maturity. Maturity was conceived as having all the trimmings of a church in the United States — a full-time pastor, a church building, an educational annex, a church office, a parsonage, committees and commissions, etc., etc. The net result of this was the creation of a top-heavy organization most of whose efforts go to support the clergy, to pay for buildings, and to keep the committees functioning, so that the churches became ingrown and lost their mission-ary zeal. Although this is obviously not true of some denomi-nations in some countries in the Latin Caribbean, it is a general statement that fairly applies to most of them.

What, then, of the relevance of these churches? It is diffi-cult to see how organizations so involved in institutional matters can be very relevant in a world that is so rapidly changing. Indeed, a large number of young people, driven to despair by their churches' irrelevance, have left them, often to join political parties' of the radical left or simply to pursue their lives in a manner they take to be more relevant to the real problems of their people. Others are working within the Church seeking to lead it to take action on the crucial issues of our times. These, however, have often been led to bitter struggles with other church leaders, and the result has been an atmosphere of misunderstanding and mistrust that pre-vents the Church from growing, being relevant, or showing the nature of reconciliation. This divisive spirit has been heightened by the false alternative between church growth and relevance, so that in many instances whole churches are being polarized between groups that argue for one or the other. The tragedy of this situation is even greater if one takes into consideration that, once again, it turns the atten-tion of the Church inwards, so that the question of growth and relevance often becomes a matter to be solved by inner ecclesiastical politics, and those who are concerned for church growth as well as those who are concerned for relevance find very little time or energy to devote to one or the other.

In spite of this, most of these churches are making a contri-bution in their own countries. Many of them, at one time or another, have provided men who have helped their countries in difficult times. Most of them are still growing, although slowly. In several of them leaders are appearing who under-stand the nature of the problems stated above, who are eagerly and sincerely looking for constructive alternatives, and who are meanwhile doing all they can to work for the reconciliation of parties within their churches.

Although there seems to be no reason to doubt that numerically the future of Protestantism in the Latin Caribbean is that of Pentecostalism, the historic churches still have a contribution to make. This contribution can follow various directions. First, they can work together with Roman Catholics and Pentecostals in an attempt to elucidate the nature of the Christian life today, for in this they have valuable insights to offer. Second, they can contribute their experience and reflection regarding the social dimensions of the gospel, when the time comes and they are asked for them. Third, and most important of all, they can offer a paradigmatic witness regarding God's purposes for modern society in the Latin Caribbean.

When the first missionaries of the historic churches began founding schools, hospitals, and other such institutions, there was little hope that their meager resources would ever make a dent in the misery of the nations in which they labored. Their action, however, proved to be a call to governments throughout the world, so that today most governments will, at least nominally, agree that public education, health, and welfare are their responsibility.

Public education, health, and welfare, however, are not the real problems of the Latin Caribbean — or of Latin America, for that matter. These problems are only a symptom of a greater evil: the lack of wealth in general and the poor distribution of that which exists. The experiences of the Latin Caribbean show that there is no easy solution to this problem. Cuba has attempted to redistribute its wealth and in its attempt has destroyed most of what it had. Puerto Rico has increased its wealth and has managed to develop a large middle class, but this has not substantially narrowed the gap between those who have and those who have not, and at the same time has made the Island more dependent than ever on American investment.

Can the historic churches not provide a witness to God's love and the power of reconciliation by creating sources of wealth that from their very beginning have the purpose of being distributed among the people? It is certain that they do not have the power to change the structures of industry and investment; but they do have the power — and the obligation — once more to be paradigmatic in their obedience in the midst of a society that is lost at the crossroads. It is also certain that they will be opposed by revolutionaries and reactionaries alike; but their early missionaries were also opposed by all sorts of witch doctors, and through the power of the Spirit were able to overcome. "If ye had faith like unto a grain of mustard seed. . . ."

# BIBLIOGRAPHY

## BOOKS

Acosta, José de. *De natura novi orbis libri duo, et De promulgatione Evangelii apud barbaros, sive De procuranda Indorum salute, libri sex*. Coloniae Agripinae: In oficina Birckmannica, 1596.

Alonso, Isidoro, and Ginés Garrido. *La Iglesia en América Central y el Caribe*. Friburgo, Suiza: Oficina Internacional de Investigaciones Científicas de FERES, 1962.

Amorim, Deolindo. *Africanismo y espiritismo*. Buenos Aires: Editorial Constancia, 1958.

Aparicio, Laurencio Angel. *Donde está el cadáver se reúnen los buitres*. Santiago de Chile: 1963.

Armas Medina, Fernando de. *Cristianización del Perú (1562-1600)*. Sevilla: Escuela de Estudios Hispano-Americanos, 1953.

Bastide, Roger. *O candomblé da Bahia*. São Paulo: Companhia editora nacional, 1961.

Bayle, Constantino. *El clero secular y la evangelización de América*. Madrid: Consejo Superior de Investigaciones Científicas, 1950.

Beaver, R. Pierce. *Ecumenical Beginnings in Protestant World Mission*. New York: Nelson, 1962.

Borges, Pedro. *Métodos misionales en la cristianización de América, siglo XVI*. Madrid: Consejo Superior de Investigaciones Científicas, 1960.

Brown, Arthur Judson. *One Hundred Years: A History of the Foreign Missionary Work of the Presbyterian Church in the U.S.A.* New York: Revell, 1936.

Considine, John Joseph. *The Church in the New Latin America*. Notre Dame, Indiana: Fides, 1964.

Courlander, Harold, and Rémy Bastien. *Religion and Politics in Haiti.* Washington: Institute for Cross-Cultural Research, 1966.

Coxill, H. Wakelin, and Kenneth Grubb, eds. *World Christian Handbook: 1962.* London: World Dominion, 1949.

Cruz Monclova, Lidio. *Historia de Puerto Rico: Siglo XIX.* 3 vols. San Juan: Editorial Universitaria, Universidad de Puerto Rico, 1957-1962.

Damboriena, Prudencio. *El protestantismo en la América Latina.* 2 vols. Friburgo, Suiza: Oficina Internacional de Investigaciones Científicas de FERES, 1963.

Detweiler, Charles Samuel. *The Waiting Isles: Baptist Mission in the Caribbean.* Philadelphia: Board of Education of the Northern Baptist Convention, 1930.

Dewart, Leslie. *Christianity and Revolution.* New York: Herder and Herder, 1963.

*Diario de la quincuagésima séptima Convocación Anual de la Iglesia Episcopal en la Diócesis Misionera de Cuba* (1965).

Díaz Acosta, Juan. *Historia de la Iglesia Evangélica Unida de Puerto Rico: Obra evangélica para el cincuentenario en Puerto Rico: 1899-1949.* San Juan: no publisher, 1949.

Egaña, Antonio de. *La teoría del Regio Vicariato español en Indias.* Roma: Analecta gregoriana, 1958.

Gibbons, William Joseph, ed. *Basic Ecclesiastical Statistics for Latin America.* Maryknoll, N. Y.: Maryknoll Publications, 1954.

Grubb, Kenneth G., and E. J. Bingle, eds. *World Christian Handbook: 1949.* London: World Dominion, 1949.

Hanke, Lewis. *The Spanish Struggle for Justice in the Conquest of America.* Philadelphia: University of Pennsylvania, 1949.

Hernáez, Francisco Javier. *Colección de Bulas, Breves y otros documentos relativos a la Iglesia de América y Filipinas.* 2 vols. Bruselas: Impr. de A. Vromant, 1879; Kraus reprint, 1964.

Herskovits, Melville Jean. *Life in a Haitian Village.* New York: Knopf, 1937.

Hoffman, Ronan. *Pioneer Theories of Missiology.* Washington: Catholic University of America, 1960.

Huxley, Francis. *The Invisibles.* London: Hart-Davis, 1966.

*Journal de la Soixante-douxième Convocation de l'Eglise Episcopale d'Haïti* (1964).

Lewis, G. K. *The American Christian Missionary Society and the Disciples of Christ.* St. Louis, Mo.: Bethany, 1937.

Loederer, Richard A. *Voodoo Fire in Haiti.* New York: Literary Guild, 1935.

Lopetegui, León, and Félix Zubillaga. *Historia de la Iglesia en la América Española: Desde el descubrimiento hasta comienzos del siglo XIX,* Vol. I: *México, América Central, Antillas.* Madrid: Biblioteca de Autores Cristianos, 1965.

Lugo, Juan L. *Pentecostés en Puerto Rico.* San Juan: Puerto Rico Gospel Press, 1951.

Mecham, John Lloyd. *Church and State in Latin America: A History of Politico-ecclesiastical Relations.* Chapel Hill, N. C.: University of North Carolina, 1934.

*Minutes of the General Assembly of the United Presbyterian Church in the United States of America, 1965.*

Neblett, Sterling Augustus. *Methodism in Cuba: The First Thirteen Years.* Macon, Georgia: Wesleyan College, 1966.

Odell, Edward Albert. *It Came to Pass.* New York: Board of National Missions, Presbyterian Church in the U.S.A., 1952.

Ortiz, Fernando. *Hampa afro-cubana; los negros brujos.* Madrid: Editorial América, 1917.

Pressoir, Catts. *Le Protestantisme Haïtien.* Port-au-Prince: Impr. de la Société biblique et des livres religieux d'Haïti, 1945-1946.

Puckett, Newbell Niles. *Folk Beliefs of the Southern Negro.* Chapel Hill, N. C.: University of North Carolina, 1926.

Sáenz, Michael. *Economic Aspects of Church Development in Puerto Rico.* Ann Arbor, Mich.: University Microfilms, 1961.

*A Short History of the Episcopal Church in Haiti.* No place nor date of publication.

Vitoria, Francisco de. *De Indis et De iure bellis ,electiones.* Ed. Ernest Nys. Washington: Carnegie, 1917.

Verger, Pierre. *Notes sur le culte des Orisa et Vodun à Bahia.* Dakar: IFAN, 1957.

Verschueren, Jan. *La République d'Haïti.* 4 vols. Wetteren, Belgique: Scaldis, 1948. Vol. I: *Panorama d'Haïti;* Vol. II: *Echos d'Haïti;* Vol. III: *Le culte du Vaudoux en Haïti;* Vol. IV: *La diocèse de Port-de-Paix.*

## ARTICLES

Altamira, R., "El texto de las Leyes de Burgos de 1512," *Revista de Historia de América,* I (1938), 5-77.

Arce Trías, M., "Consagran primer obispo nativo de la Iglesia Episcopal de Puerto Rico," *El Debate,* IV, Núm. 189 (1964), p. 3.

Badillo Bello, B., "Influencia de una Biblia," *Puerto Rico Evangélico,* 10 de Oct. de 1915, p. 17.

Bayle, Constantino, "El campo propio del sacerdote secular en la evangelización americana," *Missionalia Hispanica,* III (1946), 469-510.

————, "Ideales misioneros de los Reyes Católicos," *Missionalia Hispanica,* IX (1952), 209-231.

Biermann, B., "Das Requerimiento in der spanischen Conquista," *Neue Zeitschrift für Missionswissenschaft,* VI (1950), 94-114.

Castro Seoane, José, "La expansión de la Merced en la América colonial," *Missionalia Hispanica,* I (1944), 73-108; II (1945), 231-290.

————, "La Merced en el Perú," *Missionalia Hispanica,* III (1946), 243-320; IV (1947), 137-169, 383-401; VII (1950), 55-80.

Figueras, Antonio, "Principios de la expansión dominicana en Indias," *Missionalia Hispanica,* I (1944), 303-340.

Giménez Fernández, Manuel, "Nuevas consideraciones sobre la historia y sentido de las letras alejandrinas de 1493 referentes a las Indias," *Anuario de Estudios Americanos,* I (1944).

————, "Todavía más sobre las letras alejandrinas de 1493 referentes a las Indias," *Anales de la Universidad Hispalense,* XIV (1953), 241-301.

Lejarza, Fidel de, "Contenido misional del *Catálogo de Pasajeros a Indias,*" *Missionalia Hispanica,* I (1944), 571-582.

Lopetegui, León, "Labor misional del P. José de Acosta," *Studia Missionalia,* I (1943), 124-125.

Mateos, Francisco, "Antecedentes de la entrada de los jesuítas españoles en las misiones de América: 1538-1565," *Missionalia Hispanica,* I (1944), 109-166.

————, "Bulas portuguesas y españolas sobre descubrimientos geográficos," *Missionalia Hispanica,* XIX (1962), 5-34, 129-168.

————, "Primera expedición de misioneros jesuítas al Perú," *Missionalia Hispanica,* II (1945), 41-108.

Merino, Manuel, "La reducción de los indios a pueblos: Medio de evangelización," *Missionalia Hispanica,* III (1946), 184-194.

Sancho de Sopranis, Hipólito, "Irradiación misionera del Convento de la Merced de Jerez," *Missionalia Hispanica,* XI (1954), 5-54.

Sierra, Vicente D., "En torno a las bulas alejandrinas de 1493," *Missionalia Hispanica,* X (1953), 73-122.

————, "Y nada más sobre las bulas alejandrinas de 1493," *Missionalia Hispanica,* XII (1955), 403-428.

Valentine, Miguel A., "Antonio Badillo Hernández," *La Voz Presbiteriana,* mayo de 1960, p. 11.

## UNPUBLISHED MANUSCRIPTS AND THESES

Alard, Leopoldo J. "Proceso histórico de la Iglesia Episcopal de Cuba." At the library of the Episcopal Seminary of the Caribbean, Carolina, Puerto Rico.

Arturet, Antonio. "Desarrollo histórico de la Iglesia Evangélica Unida de Puerto Rico." At the library of the Evangelical Seminary of Puerto Rico, Río Piedras, Puerto Rico.

Burset, Victor. "The First Fifty Years of the Protestant Episcopal Church in Puerto Rico." At the library of the Episcopal Seminary of the Caribbean, Carolina, Puerto Rico.

Dalzon, W. "Coup d'oeil sur l'histoire de l'Eglise Episcopale d'Haïti: 1911-1938." At the library of the Episcopal Seminary of the Caribbean, Carolina, Puerto Rico.

Delgado, José L. "Historia de la Iglesia Bautista en Puerto Rico." At the First Baptist Church of Río Piedras, Puerto Rico.

Millien, J. E. "Une idée du premier cinquentenaire de l'Eglise Episcopale d'Haïti." At the library of the Episcopal Seminary of the Caribbean, Carolina, Puerto Rico.

Moore, Donald Troy. "Puerto Rico para Cristo. A History of the Progress of the Evangelical Missions in the Island of Puerto Rico." Doctoral dissertation presented to the Faculty of the School of Theology, Southwestern Baptist Theological Seminary, Fort Worth, Texas, 1967.

Wipfler, William L. "The Churches in the Dominican Republic in the Light of History." Thesis presented to the Faculty of Union Theological Seminary, New York, 1964.

# GENERAL INDEX